DR. WEISINGER'S ANGER WORK-OUT BOOK

By Dr. Hendrie Weisinger and Norman M. Lobsenz

NOBODY'S PERFECT
(How to Give Criticism and Get Results)

DR. WEISINGER'S ANGER WORK-OUT BOOK

HENDRIE WEISINGER, Ph.D.

QUILL / NEW YORK

For their contribution to this book, I would like to acknowledge Volcano Press and authors Daniel Sonkin and Michael Durphy. Their book is: *Learning to Live Without Violence* (1982)
Volcano Press
330 Ellis Street
San Francisco, CA 94102

The following pages include material and paragraphs from *Learning to Live Without Violence:* pages 11, 44, 45, 46, 47, 48, 49, 64, 72, 73, 76, 78, 79, 81, 83, 139, 140, 141. The author appreciates their contribution.

I would also like to acknowledge Matthew McKay, Martha Davis, and Patrick Fanning. Their book is: *Thoughts and Feelings: The Art of Cognitive Stress Intervention* (1981)
New Harbinger Publications
5674 Shattuck Avenue
Oakland, CA 94609
Chapter 13 includes material adapted from *Thoughts and Feelings.* The author appreciates their contribution.

It is the policy of William Morrow and Company, Inc., and its imprints and affiliates recognizing the importance of preserving what has been written, to print the books we publish on acid-free paper, and we exert our best efforts to that end.

Library of Congress Cataloging in Publication Data

Weisinger, Hendrie.
    Dr. Weisinger's Anger work-out book.
    Bibliography: p.
    1. Anger. 2. Health. 3. Success. I. Title.
II. Title: Anger work-out book.
BF575.A5W43   1985   152.4   85-6483
ISBN 0-688-04114-0 (pbk.)

Printed in the United States of America

30   29   28   27   26

To the memory of Jason Frederic Gruen,
who made the world a happier place

YOUR ANGER

WORK-OUTS

Introduction

Target Population

The *Anger Work-out Book* will benefit everyone!

Goal

Anger. It's the theme of the day. It is now known that millions of people experience the painful effects of anger, including cardiovascular disease, depression, obesity, low self-esteem, migraine headaches, ulcers, poor interpersonal relationships, spouse abuse, child abuse, divorce, alcoholism, drug addiction, lowered job productivity, chronic distress, and broken hearts, to name just a few.

The goal of the *Anger Work-out Book* is to stop the pain that anger brings. It gives you psychological interventions that will help you work out anger—convert it from a negative response to a creative and powerful source of energy that will improve your life. But there is a catch! Just as the athlete has to keep in shape through daily workouts, you have to keep your "self" in shape by doing the anger work-outs.

The Anger Work-outs

An anger work-out is a method to help you manage your anger. There are twenty-two work-outs and they combine to give you the most powerful means known for dealing with your anger and the anger of others. All the work-outs are based on empirical research (see Bibliography) and have been validated by thousands of mental health workers, business men and women, teachers, and individuals like yourself. In short, they work!

All twenty-two work-outs are self-contained; doing any of them will give you valuable anger-management skills. You may do them in any order. The first page of each work-out will tell you whom it is recommended for so that you can immediately do the work-outs in accordance with your own priorities. An important point is that the skills you develop from each work-out will help you in every aspect of your life, not just in your ability to work out anger. This is one reason why the book benefits everyone, even people who feel they are able to manage their anger.

Each work-out is organized into three sections: Purpose, Information, and Take Action. *Purpose* explains the rationale for the specific work-out, how it helps in working out anger and the benefits you will receive if you complete the work-out. *Information* provides you with knowledge that will improve your work-out skills. As you go through the information, you will come across numerous Work-out Tips and Work-out Notes. Work-out Tips will tell you how to make working out your anger easier. Here is an example of a workout tip:

INCLUDE YOUR LOVER IN THE WORK-OUT PROCESS

Work-out Notes highlight, clarify, and elaborate on the information presented in each work-out. Although reading the Work-out Notes is not essential, it is recommended since the more you know about anger, the easier it becomes to manage your anger productively. Here is an example of a work-out note:

W O R K - O U T   N O T E

There are dozens of theories and thousands of empirical studies seeking to explain why people have low self-esteem, are obese, depressed, alcoholic, drug addicted, suffer from migraine headaches and ulcers, develop sexual dysfunctions, lose jobs and friends, abuse their spouses and children, are prone to heartbreak and heart attacks, and become suicidal. A consistent finding is that people who adopt these self-destructive patterns have an inability to work out their anger. Certainly, anger is not the sole cause in any of these ailments, but its constant appearance indicates that it's a prime cause in almost all of them.

Until intelligent thought is linked with appropriate action and follow-through, there is no real accomplishment. Therefore, at the end of the information, you will be asked to Take Action. *Taking action* involves the mechanics of working out anger and is based on the assumption that man by nature is not a passive recipient of the events life throws at him. He is active in shaping his own destiny but may respond to his environment in ways that are not always beneficial. All of us have developed counterproductive patterns for dealing with anger. These patterns will persist unless we actively change them by becoming a directive force. The best way to do this is to take action. Each time you take action, you implement the psychological interventions that help you work out. Nothing takes the place of action. Taking action moves you through the work-out process.

All Take Actions have the following characteristics:

1. They are concrete activities. They tell you specifically what to do and how to do it.
2. They are current. You can do them immediately, not next week.
3. They are in your control. You need not depend on others for success.

When you take action, you are doing your anger exercise, applying the work-out information.

You will also learn the biggest mistake that people make in each of the twenty-two work-outs. Knowing the mistakes makes it easier to avoid them.

Using the Anger Work-out Book

The *Anger Work-out Book* is a self-action book, a participative book designed to create change, not just intellectual insight. The best way to use it is by involving yourself in *doing* the work-outs, not just reading about them. One way to make sure you are participating behaviorally is to write in your book. At times, you may think writing down your responses serves no purpose. However, research has shown that people who write down productive actions to take, in contrast to those who only keep them in mind, are much more likely to act on them. What you write in each work-out will also serve as valuable information that will help you do the other work-outs. The point to remember is that although this is a workbook, you must make it work for you by using it.

Do not rush through this book. Take your time. A few days, a week, or even longer may be spent on any of the work-outs. Many people want to read the book very quickly and this is also all right as long as you remember to go back to each work-out and take action. The important thing is to move through the work-out process experimentally.

A key point to remember is that the work-out process is ongoing. When you stop doing any of the work-outs, your old counterproductive anger habits are likely to reemerge. The more you work out, the less chance there is to be hurt by your old anger habits. Eventually, you will be able to do the work-outs on an automatic basis. When this happens you will be an anger athlete and will be more productive in all aspects of your life. You will be a more loving person, a better parent, a more effective worker—and will live longer. Working out your anger shapes you up!

A DEFINITION OF ANGER

Everybody has his or her own definition of *anger*. *Webster's New World Dictionary* defines it as a noun meaning a feeling of displeasure resulting from injury, mistreatment, opposition, and usually showing itself in a desire to fight back at the supposed cause of this feeling.

The WORK-OUT PROCESS defines anger as:

- an *emotion*. It is physically arousing and it has unique physiological correlates.
- a *feeling*. It has an effect on the way you experience your world.
- a *communicator*. It sends information to others.
- a *cause*. It produces specific effects and results.

THINK ABOUT *YOUR* DEFINITION OF ANGER.

ANGER WORK-OUT #1
Looking Good

Recommended for:
1. *People who want to be more aware of their anger*
2. *People who want to cut out or improve a specific behavior*
3. *People who want to succeed in any self-help program*

PURPOSE

Looking at how you handle anger is essential to the work-out process because it lets you know how you are responding, the progress you are making, and what you need to do to work out your anger.

Anger Work-out #1 will help you learn the skill of self-monitoring (SM), accurately observing your own behavior. Observing and recording your own specific behavior helps immediately because you become more aware of its occurrence. You also have objective evidence of the change in your monitored behavior over time. Thus, self monitoring is *reactive*—just doing it will alter the behavior you wish to change.

Self-monitoring is also built into all of the other work-outs. If you can learn to do it well now, all the other work-outs will become easier and more effective. For these reasons, begin to self-monitor your anger right now.

WORK-OUT NOTE

Of all psychological skills, self-monitoring best reflects the megatrend of moving from institutional help to self-help. It is the core skill that all self-help programs rely on. Unfortunately, almost all self-help programs assume that people know how to self-monitor their behavior and are able to do it—an assumption that is refuted by empirical research—and therefore neglect to teach people how to do it. The work-out process is an exception.

INFORMATION

Practice Makes Perfect

Like any skill, self-monitoring requires practice. First, increase your *awareness* of the how, what, or when of certain behavior. A good way to practice is to choose very simple, general, and obvious behaviors that you have no desire to actually change. As your skill in watching yourself increases, you can move on to behaviors that you *want* to change.

Measuring and recording your behavior

After you have selected a behavior to self-monitor, you have to decide *how* you will measure and record its occurrence. There are two ways to measure your behavior's occurrence:

- Frequency—how many times you do the behavior
- Time interval—how long you do the behavior

Some behaviors, such as smoking, lend themselves to a frequency count, whereas others, such as studying, are measured best by using time intervals. Other behaviors, such as arguing with your spouse, may be measured by both methods.

Once you determine how you will measure your selected behavior, you have to devise a method for recording it unobtrusively and conveniently: This method must be available wherever and whenever the behavior occurs. Recording your behavior is crucial to self-monitoring because it "forces" you to observe yourself accurately. Here are some suggestions for making frequency counts.

- A golf counter worn like a wristwatch to count the times you do each behavior

- Transferring a penny from one pocket to another each time you do the behavior
- Carrying a small pad and pencil and writing down an _X_ each time you do the behavior

For a time interval, the best method of recording is to clock the beginning and ending times and then immediately write the duration down.

Keeping accurate records

Regardless of how you record your behavior, it is imperative that you transfer your data to a written record at a regular time, for instance, before you go to bed. Keeping a daily data sheet gives you objective evidence of the changes you are making. Just note the day and the number of times (or average length of time) the behavior occurs. If you fail to keep a daily data sheet, you will have to rely on your memory, which research has shown to be an inaccurate method for self-monitoring.

Visualizing your data

After you have transferred your recorded data to your daily data sheet, your next task is to visualize it. This is important because it lets you _see_ the actual changes that are being made and helps perpetuate changes in the desired direction. Visualizing your progress gives you support, motivation, and recognition and proves that you _can_ change. Visualization is facilitated by transforming the data into a graph. Simply plot your data on the grid and connect the lines at the end of each day. The _slope_ of the line illustrates the change in the frequency of the behavior. Ideally, a graph at the end of a week would take this shape (for a behavior you want to decrease).

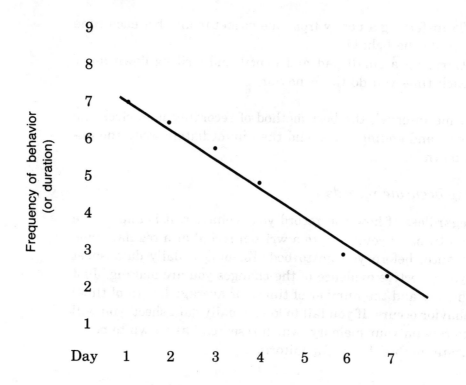

Self-Monitoring Your Anger

After you have practiced self-monitoring, you are ready to begin the process of self-monitoring your anger. Because you are just starting to work out, the easiest behavior for you to self-monitor is the *frequency* of your anger, which will cause a reduction in the number of times you experience destructive anger each day. Observing the frequency of your anger will have positive effects on other aspects of your anger. As you become more skilled in self-monitoring, and move through the work out process, it will be easier for you to self-monitor more subtle aspects of your anger, such as destructive things you say to yourself when you are angry that make you angrier (counterproductive self-statements) and your physiological changes. Inevitably—if you continue to work out—you will be able to self-monitor many aspects of your anger simultaneously.

Getting Validated

Crucial to the self-monitoring process is accurately recording the behavior when you do it. Sometimes, even with good intentions, we fail to do this because we do not acknowledge we are really doing the behavior. For example, a dieter may not count a piece of candy because he took only a tiny bite, or the smoker may not count his one or two puffs as really smoking. These behaviors go uncounted and give the individual an inaccurate perception of the actual frequency of the behavior in question. This is especially common with anger because a major way of dealing with it is to deny it for whatever reason. Thus, you may in fact be angry, but may not want to admit it to yourself. Therefore, you will not record it.

One way in which you can increase the chances that you are accurately perceiving and recording the times you do get angry is to use the technique of consensual validation. This means asking another person to monitor your behavior *independent* of your own monitoring. If there is a wide discrepency between your self-monitoring and their observations, use the difference not to start an argument but as a cue that perhaps you are not acknowledging your anger every time you get angry. The closer your agreement, the more you can be sure that you are accurately monitoring the frequency of your anger.

Obviously, it would be very difficult to get someone to follow you around and watch you all the time, but don't let that stop you. Arrange for someone to make spot checks for designated periods. At the end of the time period, they share with you their perceptions of your behavior and you are able to check them against your self-monitoring. Since your anger affects other people, you will find that many people will consent to validate you. Here is a procedure for getting validated.

- Select a person whom you trust and frequently spend time with. If possible, use your spouse, lover, or roommate.
- Explain to them that you are working out and would appreciate their help in monitoring the number of times they think you get angry during the next two weeks.
- Give them an unobtrusive and convenient means for measuring and recording the frequency of your anger.
- Instruct them to monitor the frequency of your anger when they are with you, and to mentally record the specifics of the situation. At the end of the day, or of time spent together, ask them to give you their count immediately.

- Check to see if their count is the same as yours, and if the anger incidents were the same.
- When they perceive your anger more frequently than you do, ask for details as to *how* they perceived your anger. Use their input to increase your awareness.

As the accuracy of your self-monitoring is validated more and more, you will have less need to be validated because you will know that your self-monitoring is accurate. When this happens, you will be looking good!

W O R K - O U T   N O T E

At times, the validator may want to tell the monitored person immediately when he thinks she is angry. Be aware that while sometimes appropriate, this response frequently initiates an escalating pattern.

TAKE ACTION

1. Choose one behavior from the following list, making sure the one you choose is not something you want to change. (Your goal is to practice watching yourself, not to change your behavior.) Next to the behavior you choose, write how you will measure it (frequency or interval).

   Going to the bathroom_____

   Making telephone calls_____

   Watching television_____

   Self-monitor your selected behavior for five days. At the end of each day, transfer your data into a graph. To make it easier for you, here are your daily data sheet and graph grid already prepared.

Days	1	2	3	4	5	6	7	8	9	10
Number of times or average length of time the behavior occurred	—	—	—	—	—	—	—	—	—	—

Number of times or average length of time the behavior occurred

10
9
8
7
6
5
4
3
2
1

Days	1	2	3	4	5	6	7	8	9	10

2. After you have practiced self-monitoring, begin to self-monitor the frequency of your anger for at least ten days (the longer, the better). Measure your data by moving pennies or matchsticks from one pocket to another, or by using some other way that is *convenient* for you. To make it easier for you, here are your daily data sheet and graph grid already prepared.

Days	1	2	3	4	5	6	7	8	9	10
Number of times you got angry	—	—	—	—	—	—	—	—	—	—

Number of times you got angry

10
9
8
7
6
5
4
3
2
1

Days	1	2	3	4	5	6	7	8	9	10

3. Get Validated.

THE BIGGEST MISTAKE PEOPLE MAKE
IN THIS WORK-OUT IS

to fail to measure or record their behavior because they are lazy and/or do not believe that self-monitoring really works. Self-monitoring is not a pop psychology gimmick. It is a proven method to decrease undesirable behavior and increase desirable behavior. Do it and you will see this to be true.

W O R K - O U T   N O T E S

_____

_____

_____

_____

_____

_____

_____

_____

_____

_____

ANGER WORK-OUT #2

Your Work-out Suit

PURPOSE

Anger Work-out #2 will familiarize you with three essential *emotional* components of anger: thoughts, bodily responses, and behavior. Skill in managing these components will help you control your anger, a prerequisite for working it out. Anger Work-out #2 is the most technical work-out, so take your time doing it.

WORK-OUT NOTE

An important assumption of the work-out process is that the full experience of anger (an emotional state) must include a fusion of thoughts, actions, and somatic reactions. When these components are dissociated, we are left with something other than a true "anger state"—e.g., frustration or hurt. The work-out process utilizes this point.

INFORMATION

Thinking About Anger

Many types of thoughts affect anger but the most important ones come from a type of thinking process called cognitive appraisal. This is the mental process that helps us define and interpret what is happening to or around us. Its roots lie in special qualities and circumstances—family background, natural talents, physical appearance, systems of belief—that help us shape our personalities. These combine to form the basis for the unique way each of us appraises the situations we encounter in daily life.

The way we *appraise* our environment at any given moment is crucial in determining how we respond emotionally. While this thought is hardly original (Epictetus said two thousand years ago, "Men are not troubled by things themselves, but by their thoughts about them"), psychologists today agree that it is the meaning we assign to events that gives them the power to affect us for good or ill. Here are some facts about cognitive appraisal as they relate to working out anger:

- The cognitive (thinking) activity in appraisal does not imply anything about deliberate reflection, rationality, or awareness.

When we are angry, the appraisals that we make are frequently distorted, influencing us to act in what appears to others a highly irrational way. "He got out of control," we say. "He wasn't thinking. If he had been, he wouldn't have acted *that* way." But he was thinking. In other words, the process of appraisal—independent of how it is used—is continually in use, and you are continually using it.

The work-out process takes advantage of the appraisal process by improving your *appraisal skills* so that you can use them to assess, manage, and strategically direct anger for productive gains.

WORK-OUT NOTE

Unfortunately, it is a widespread belief that *cognition* is rational whereas *feeling* is irrational and primitive, a view that goes back to classical Greek times and that was also emphasized by the Catholic Church during the Middle Ages. Even today, most psychologists treat emotions as primitive, midbrain phenomena, whereas reason is seen to reflect human phylogenetic superiority and as vulnerable to being overwhelmed by the primitivizing effects of passion. One of the most influential schools of psychotherapy argues, in accord with this centuries-old tradition, that faulty belief premises underlie psychopathology, creating distressing emotional states when the person reacts to situations on the basis of such premises. The therapy is designed to help the person give up the faulty beliefs so that he or she can operate more effectively and with less misery. However, the view is growing that even positively toned, healthy emotions such as joy, peacefulness, love, and certainly many human commitments that sustain morale, rest on shared or private illusions and depend on beliefs whose accuracy is often irrelevant to the elicitation of the emotion. The point is that cognition cannot be equated with rationality. The cognitive appraisals that shape our emotional reactions can distort reality as well as reflect it realistically.

• Different people can appraise the *same* event differently.

You and your lover may appraise the same situation in contrary ways, which typically leads to conflict. Since our perceptions are always individual, it is improbable that the appraisals of two people will ever completely coincide. An oversized sofa, for example, will have different implications for an upholsterer, a couple in love, a decorator, a mover. Seat four people at a card table and place a block *M* on it. Depending on their positions they will see it as an *M,* an *E,* a *W* or an angular *3*.

Similarly, anger between people is often the result of "mentally sitting" in a different seat. Each individual may feel that his or her viewpoint is the only correct one, depending on their cognitive appraisals.

The work-out process stresses that you use the fact that *different people appraise things differently* as a means for understanding and resolving conflict. In short, the work-out process clarifies not only where you are "sitting" when you get angry, but of equal importance, where the other guy's chair is too.

• We can appraise the *same* event differently at different times.

Frequently, we respond to events with intense anger, emotionally hurting ourselves and perhaps others. We usually end up saying "I'm not angry anymore" or "I thought about it and you're right," which lets the others involved know that our wrath has been extinguished. The typical response is "Forget it; it's all right," which lets us know that they too are happy that the fire is out.

Essential to the work-out process is being aware of what it *is* that puts the fire out. The speeding ticket you got on your way home still has to be paid the next day, but the anger may have subsided. The antique vase your child accidentally broke is still broken, but later the anger disappears. Obviously, the event has not changed but the way we appraise it does.

WORK-OUT NOTE

As we have seen, the process of appraisal is ongoing. Each appraisal provides information that, whether it is accurate or distorted, affects the way we respond to our environment. Unfortunately, we cannot and do not always wait around to collect all the information we need, spend the time necessary to analyze and assess it, and then act accordingly. In this sense, humans are like the rabbit that psychologist Zajonic describes:

> The rabbit cannot stop to contemplate the length of the snake's fangs or the geometry of its markings. If the rabbit is to escape, the action must be undertaken long before . . . the rabbit has fully established and verified that a nearby movement might reveal a snake in all its coiled glory. The decision to run must be made on the basis of *minimal cognitive engagement.*

We humans are also forced to use *minimal cognitive engagement.* Not having enough information, and not taking the time to collect more or appraise it accurately, we make our response on what we do have, even if it is inaccurate and incomplete. As a consequence, our actions are frequently judged to be irrational and unfair. This process—acting on decisions that are based on incomplete information and/or not enough time to accurately appraise a situation—is a major factor in creating destructive anger—anger that is justified not by the reality of the situation but by our distorted perceptions. Only when we gather more information, or reappraise what we do have, do we show a "change of heart." We are appraising the same event differently. The fact that we are able to do this, and that we know *how* to do it, is one of the qualities that enable us to change our anger styles.

The work-out process teaches you not to be victimized by minimal cognitive engagement. It teaches you how to gather information and how to accurately appraise it. The work-out process teaches *maximum* cognitive engagement. As a result, you will be able to cut down on the times you get angry needlessly and unjustly.

The better you become at appraising situations accurately, the *easier* it will become to work out your anger.

WHEN YOU ARE ANGRY, LOOK FOR ALTERNATIVE APPRAISALS OF THE EVENT.

Your Body Changes

When I'm angry, I feel_____.
If you are like the thirty-five hundred men, women, and children who completed this sentence in research for this book your answer probably includes one or more of the following:

mad
upset
hurt
boiling
good
as if I want to hit someone
like I want to run away

Responses such as these illustrate that we habitually describe anger in terms of feelings. Rarely do we describe anger in terms of physiology. The work-out process stresses that you must become aware of your body's physiology, or to be more exact, the *somatic disturbances* that your anger creates.

Somatic disturbances, the changes that occur in your body when you experience anger, constitute *anger arousal,* which is the second necessary component of experiencing anger.

Emotions are thought to have distinct physiological characteristics as well as mental and behavioral ones. Research has demonstrated that anger changes your body in predictable ways and that frequent anger arousal is clearly detrimental. For example, anger arousal causes increased heart rate and blood pressure; this sets off a chain reaction in your normal physiology, making you more prone to heart problems, essential hypertension, and other illnesses that affect the quality of your life. *The work-out process will help reduce the bodily distress that anger creates, thus improving your physical and mental health.*

Furthermore, when you get angry, anger arousal occurs "automatically." You breathe harder and faster, you feel palpitation, and your blood pressure soars. Any attempt you make to control yourself is after the fact and is like throwing a bucket of water on a blazing fire. When the damage is done, little helps. Even the spouse or friend trying to calm you when you are extremely angry (aroused) may aggravate matters. For example,

"Honey, calm down."
"Don't tell me what to do, damn it!"

The work-out process will help control the fire by teaching you how to use anger arousal as a *cue* that something is wrong and that it is time to work out. *The work-out process will teach you how to take advantage of anger arousal by using it as a source of energy to help you act productively.* The more adept you become in identifying your anger arousal, the *faster* you can start to work out.

Anger Actions

It is our actions that communicate to others that we are angry at them and vice versa. Actions, then, are the third necessary component of emotionally experiencing anger.

Anger actions are those behavioral patterns that make our anger more destructive. Yelling is a good example. Understanding how anger actions arise and work is another part of the work-out process.

Understanding your behavior and why you do the things you do does not require psychoanalysis. It just means familiarizing yourself with some basic psychological learning principles. Two learning principles that affect you every day are modeling and operant learning.

Modeling

Psychological research has taught us that observing other people can teach us what to do and how to do it. The son who learns to knot his tie by watching his father is usually modeling. The mother who teaches her daughter to crack an egg by saying, "Watch me first," is using modeling. The young musician who watches his favorite entertainer and then goes onstage and does likewise is using modeling too.

Unfortunately, in the case of anger, we frequently model behavior that is counterproductive to ourselves and to others.

Think back to how your parents and significant others in your childhood expressed anger. Chances are that if your parents expressed anger by yelling and slamming the door, you probably do the same. If your parents went into different parts of the house at angry moments, your anger actions probably include leaving the scene in a hurry or ignoring the other person, rather than face-to-face combat. In both cases, you have *learned* actions for expressing anger by observing how others act. You have modeled their behavior. As in the case of appraisal, the way we model is not always in our best interest.

Operant learning

Innumerable psychological studies demonstrate that we learn to act in ways that lead to certain results. This is called *operant learning* because our behavior "operates" on our environment (or another person) to produce specific results—we make a response, and then we see what it brings. If the response we make brings desirable results, we tend to repeat it because it gets *reinforced*. If the results of our actions are unwanted, or not reinforced, we stop doing it, or respond differently.

Examples of operant learning are all around us. The child learns to throw a Frisbee by throwing it in different ways until he discovers the way to pitch it with accuracy. He then knows how and can do it again. Finding the right way to hold a baby so it won't cry is operant learning. Mixing a recipe to taste is operant learning too. Sometimes we get the result we want on the first try. Other times, we try a hundred responses before we get what we want. But in any case, the response that we "keep" is the response that gets us what we want.

Many of us have learned our anger actions through operant learning. For example, a man may learn that if he doesn't want to hear his wife's complaints, all he has to do is insult her and she will quickly retreat to her magazines. The fact that his wife always acts in the same way serves to increase the probability that he will insult her in the future whenever she voices her complaints. Although his insulting actions are hardly productive for their relationship, he does get a desirable result—his wife stops nagging him. His wife similarly "learns" that if she communicates her anger by withdrawing, she won't have to hear his insults. Her anger actions get a "desirable result" too. Because they both get what they want, at least temporarily, their actions will tend to be repeated. For them, reinforcing each other's behavior will probably lead to a divorce.

Operant learning, like modeling, does help us acquire new behaviors, but not necessarily productive ones.

The work-out process will teach you how to use the principles of modeling and operant learning to change anger actions into productive behavior that will bring positive results.

Ability to identify your anger actions will make it *easier* for you to know what behaviors are destructive. These behaviors can then be changed by working out.

How Anger Works

Anger involves a complex system of reactions that includes thinking, bodily changes, and behavior. To know *how* anger works we have to understand how this system works—what initiates it, and what perpetuates it.

Knowing how anger works will help you in several ways:

- In any given situation, you will be in a better position to work out your anger.
- You will recognize how you perpetuate your anger in a counterproductive manner and know *what* to change to make it productive.
- You will understand and deal more effectively with the anger of others.

To understand how anger works, remember that events have no emotional value per se. The process of cognitive appraisal gives meaning to those events. Depending on the intensity of the appraisal, we experience a shift in our level of physiological arousal, which then, in conjunction with our thinking, causes us to act in a certain way. When we appraise a situation in an "angry manner," the shift in physiological arousal becomes anger arousal and the behavior that follows becomes our anger actions.

Sometimes it seems that the first thing we become aware of is anger arousal, rather than angry thoughts. Academicians debate whether thoughts precede bodily changes or vice versa. Some even take the position that behavior comes before thought or somatic changes. It serves no purpose to get caught up in the chicken or the egg debate; we should simply recognize that anger is produced by an interaction (fusion) of our thoughts, bodily changes, and behavior that is triggered by external events that tend to make us angry. These external events are known as *provocations*.

The traditional result of the way we respond to a provocation is an *anger feeedback loop* that is made up of our thoughts, bodily changes, and behavior. Each influences and reacts with the others in an escalating manner. For example, you "appraise" your child's failure to put his toys away as a deliberate disobedience. This appraisal leads to angry thoughts; "He never listens to me, damn it. The kid's a real problem." Your body reacts to these thoughts with a typical anger arousal response: pounding heart, tightened gut, increased pulse. You interpret (appraise) this arousal as further evidence of anger, thinking, "Boy, this really pisses me off." Your body gets the message that you *are* angry, and next thing you know, you are either yelling at your child or storming out of the room. Observing your "self" doing these angry actions not only supports your thinking and arousal that you are indeed angry, but also intensifies each reaction. In short, a vicious system is in motion.

The following diagram illustrates the process of anger.

HOW (EMOTIONAL) ANGER WORKS

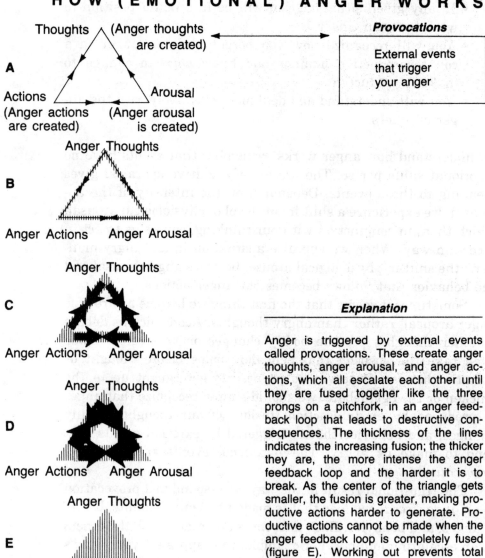

Provocations

External events that trigger your anger

Explanation

Anger is triggered by external events called provocations. These create anger thoughts, anger arousal, and anger actions, which all escalate each other until they are fused together like the three prongs on a pitchfork, in an anger feedback loop that leads to destructive consequences. The thickness of the lines indicates the increasing fusion; the thicker they are, the more intense the anger feedback loop and the harder it is to break. As the center of the triangle gets smaller, the fusion is greater, making productive actions harder to generate. Productive actions cannot be made when the anger feedback loop is completely fused (figure E). Working out prevents total fusion.

Our own thoughts, bodily changes, and behavior perpetuate anger—not someone else's actions or an external event. Saying "You make me angry" is self-defeating. As long as you blame your anger on someone else or a daily happening that you encountered, you give up the chance to change how *you* respond. Acknowledging the fact that *you* perpetuate your anger creates the possibility of dealing with provocation more productively.

The potential anger athlete will ask, "Since we can always interpret a situation in several ways, what is it that predisposes us toward an 'anger appraisal' (or anger arousal or anger actions)?" The work-out process posits that you are predisposed to experience anger when you appraise an event or a person as a threat to one of your basic needs such as food or shelter or more mature needs such as identity, recognition, achievement, and social affiliation.

Because the process of cognitive appraisal is not always rational, we frequently misinterpret a provocation as being a threat to one of our needs. Such cognitive distortions—perceptions that our needs are being threatened—are known as *hot cognitions* because they elicit anger arousal. They are thoughts *with* feelings. Hot cognitions make us experience strong doses of anger needlessly and have a bewildering and disturbing effect on others as well as ourselves:

"What's he so angry about? I just don't understand him."

"I'm really afraid of his temper. I never know when he will explode."

"I'm getting an ulcer over this."

Since the predominant way humans respond to a threat is anger, the greater the distortion (greater than the perceived threat), the more likely is *intense anger* to result.

angry destructive self-statements

"I'll kill the s.o.b."

INTENSE ANGER: *self-destructive anger arousal*

heart attack

destructive anger actions

yelling, running out of the house,
silent treatment

Thus, the man who "appraises" his wife's being late to his office party as ruining his chances for promotion (a threat to his needs of recognition and security) is apt to experience anger more intensely than his counterpart who thinks, "Big deal, I'm upset but it's not the worst thing in the world." The latter appraisal is not a hot cognition. The woman who gets angry when her husband ignores her is perhaps making the hot cognition that her need for intimacy is being threatened. She will be angrier than the woman who interprets her husband's passive listening to his simply being bored about the topic at hand.

If we can put our provocations in perspective and see that they do not threaten our basic needs, we can keep our anger at a moderate level and use its "dynamite power" to get productive results. If we fail to do this, we create the anger feedback loop.

To break an anger loop, then, you have to do the following:

- Be able to identify and understand your provocations, for these are the external events that interact with your thoughts, bodily changes, and behavior to *initiate* your anger.
- Be able to change your thoughts, physical responses, and actions that are perpetuating your anger.
- Initiate and substitute productive ways of dealing with your anger.

THIS IS EXACTLY THE PURPOSE OF THE ANGER
WORK-OUT PROCESS

Knowing how your thoughts, bodily changes, and actions work together is crucial for emotionally controlling your anger. Together, they are your three-piece work-out suit. Be sure to wear it well.

TAKE ACTION

1. List an event that you are still angry about and next to it write down how you appraise it. Then write down an alternative appraisal, perhaps reflecting the other person's view (if one is involved). Think about your alternative appraisal and observe the effect it has on your anger.

    Anger incident:_____

    How you appraise it:_____

    Alternate appraisal:_____

2. List the somatic disturbances that you are now aware of when you are angry and begin to use them as a cue that it is time to work out. Take a deep breath when you notice them.

    _____   _____

    _____   _____

    _____   _____

3. List the actions you *do* when you are angry and check the ones that are anger actions.

    _____   _____

    _____   _____

    _____   _____

4. List two things you can do when you get angry instead of your anger action.

    _____

    _____

THE BIGGEST MISTAKE PEOPLE MAKE
IN THIS WORK-OUT IS

not to spend enough time thinking about the work-out's content. Thus, they fail to appreciate the importance of having a good work-out suit, let alone wearing it.

W O R K - O U T   N O T E S

_____

_____

_____

_____

_____

_____

_____

_____

_____

_____

ANGER WORK-OUT #3

The Good, the Bad, and the Ugly

PURPOSE

Here are four important questions that you need to be able to answer if you are to work out your anger:

1. When is your anger valid?
2. When is your anger needless?
3. When is your anger just?
4. When is your anger a problem?

The answers will help you understand how your anger is currently affecting your life. You can then learn how to *use* your anger to improve your life.

INFORMATION

When Your Anger Is Valid

Your anger is ugly, but it is *always* valid. Anger is an emotion and a feeling. And like all emotions and feelings, it is your human right to experience it. Rather than feeling guilty about getting angry, or arguing about whether or not you have the right to be angry, focus on accepting and validating your anger, acknowledging to yourself that you *are* angry.

Validating your anger prevents you from trying to suppress or deny your anger. Validating your anger also helps you learn to validate your other feelings. In a sense, it helps you "feel" your feelings and enables you to grow emotionally. Failure to validate your anger affects you in counterproductive ways. Remember, anger cannot be stuffed. One way you can validate your anger is simply to say, "I am angry now." Another way is to write your feelings down.

BEGIN TO VALIDATE YOUR LOVER'S ANGER.

When Your Anger Is Needless or Adaptive

Needless anger is bad anger because it doesn't do you any good. In fact, it makes matters worse. A simple way to tell if your anger is needless is to ask yourself the question:

"Is my anger helping me in this situation?"

If the answer is no, your anger is needless in the sense that you need to develop a more productive response to achieve your goal.

An important point to recognize is that anger is frequently needless because of the way you *use* it. For example, to get upset because a friend canceled plans at the last minute is not going to change the situation, nor is it going to make you feel better. Sitting home and stewing is needless. On the other hand, if you can use your anger as a source of energy to psyche yourself up to tell your friend how you feel about their breaking plans at the last moment or to go out and enjoy yourself, then your anger is far from needless—it is adaptive. If you get angry over your inability to do a task and decide to throw in the towel, your anger will no doubt lead to feelings of low self-esteem. But if you can use your anger as energy to increase your determination, you will eventually finish the task at hand and increase your self-esteem. Again, your anger is adaptive.

Knowing whether or not your anger is needless is important because it helps you see how you "use" your anger. Familiarizing yourself with the positive and negative functions of anger will help you know when your anger is needless, or to be more exact, when you need less anger.

Anger's Positive Functions	*Anger's Negative Functions*
Anger is an *energizer*. It gives us vigor, mobilizes the body's resources for self-defense, and provides us with stamina when a task gets difficult. It enables us to deal with conflict by supplying the fuel for the fight.	Anger can disrupt our thoughts and actions. When angry, it is harder to think clearly and evaluate options. It causes us to act impulsively without considering the consequences of our behavior.
Anger can be helpful in *expressing* tension and communicating our negative feelings to others. The productive expression of anger is an important way to resolve conflict.	Sometimes anger is a way to defend ourselves when it is not necessary. When we get hurt or embarrassed we can get angry as a way to protect our pride. It is easier to be angry than to be anxious. Anger used like this prevents us from recognizing our feelings and facing ourselves.
Anger gives us information about people and situations. It serves as a *cue* to tell us that there is something unjust, frustrating, threatening, or annoying going on. It can be a signal that tells us it is time to cope with the distress.	Anger can *instigate* or lead to aggression. When we become emotionally upset, we sometimes try to discharge or release our feelings through our behavior—we get angry and then try to take it out on something or someone.
Anger arousal can *potentiate* a feeling of control. When a situation is getting out of hand, converting anger arousal into energy enables us to take charge and assert our will or interest.	Anger can convey a negative impression to others. It can cause contempt, fear, avoidance, repudiation.

You can begin to cut down on needless anger by minimizing your anger's negative functions, and by using its positive functions.

**IN SITUATIONS YOU CAN'T CHANGE, USE YOUR ANGER
TO PREVENT THEM FROM RECURRING.**

When Your Anger Is Just

Knowing when your anger is *just* is important because it helps you feel better about the times you are angry instead of feeling guilty, embarrassed, or ashamed or experiencing other distressful feelings.

"Just anger" means that you have a right to "attack" (talk to) what you consider the provocation. It means that your anger is reasonably well grounded (free of cognitive distortions), and that other people would probably be angry in the same situation. Asking yourself the following question is a good guideline for judging whether your anger is just:

"Is my anger directed toward someone who has knowingly, intentionally, and unnecessarily acted in a hurtful manner?"

When you can answer yes, your anger has good cause. Here are some examples of what most people consider clear cases of just and unjust anger:

Just Anger	Unjust Anger
Spouse or friend lies to you.	Your spouse gets home late because of being stuck in traffic.
Boss embarrasses you in front of others.	Someone accidentally pushes you or dents your car.
A friend betrays you.	Your kids make too much noise while playing.
You are abused.	
Someone promises to do something and then doesn't.	

In the just situation, your anger is triggered by the intentional actions of someone else. In the unjust situation your anger is triggered either by your own "hot cognitions," or by the actions of someone who did not intend to upset you (kids playing).

If you find that most of your anger is just, then you are using it well—as a source of energy to help you defend yourself from being abused or treated unfairly. But even if your anger is just, it does not mean that the way you express it is just. For example, your spouse may lie to you but yelling at him or hitting her is certainly not a just response. Once you know that your anger is just, your next step becomes learning how to express it in a just manner. Check out (and work out) Anger Work-out #6.

If you find that most of your anger is unjust, then your anger is a destructive force in your life.

Study the chart below so you will know when your anger is valid, needless or adaptive, just or unjust.

Valid	*Needless or Adaptive*	*Just or Unjust*
Anger, like all feelings and emotions, is always valid.	Anger is needless when it hurts you. It is adaptive when it helps you.	Anger is just when you have been intentionally hurt or treated unfairly (and others would agree). It is unjust when you "attack" a person whose intent is not to hurt you or be unfair to you. It is your hot cognitions that create the anger.

W O R K - O U T   N O T E

Just anger and needless anger should not be thought of as being on opposite ends of the same continuum. As the preceding chart indicates, the opposite of needless anger is adaptive anger, while the opposite of just anger is unjust anger. Anger can be unjust but still adaptive. For example, if your boss fires you because of incompetency, your resulting anger (while valid) is certainly not just. But if you can use your anger as energy to go out and get another job, even a better one, your anger is adaptive. Similarly, just anger can easily lead to needless anger. For example, your anger is justified because your mother deliberately makes cutting remarks that cause you constant emotional distress. Anger athletes use this anger as a cue that their relationship with their mother is in trouble and needs direct attention. For others, the just anger becomes a reason to become angrier. This creates needless anger because the extra anger makes things worse. They end up yelling at their mother or not talking to her for long periods of time. They need less anger.

When Your Anger Is a Problem

At one time or another, everyone experiences needless and unjust anger. But too much of either makes anger a problem. Here are five specific signals that will tell you when your anger is creating problems for you.

1. *When it is too frequent.* There are many situations for which becoming angry is justified and proper. However,

we often get angry when it is not necessary or useful. You must begin to make a distinction between the times when it is all right to be angry and when getting angry isn't such a good idea.

2. *When it is too intense.* Anger is something that occurs at different levels of intensity. A small or moderate amount of anger can often work to your advantage. But high degrees of anger seldom produce positive results.

3. *When it lasts too long.* When anger is prolonged, you maintain a level of arousal or stress that goes beyond normal limits. We often think of this as "making too much of something." When anger does not subside, your body's systems are prevented from returning to normal levels, making you susceptible to further aggravation and annoyance. It becomes easier to get angry the next time something goes wrong. Furthermore, when anger lasts too long, resolution of conflict becomes more difficult and eventually impossible.

4. *When it leads to aggression.* Aggressive acts are sure to get you into trouble. When you feel you have been abused or treated unfairly, you may want to lash out at the person who has offended you. Anger, particularly when intense and personal, pushes for an aggressive response. Your muscles get tense, your voice gets louder, and you clench your fists and stare sharply. There is then a greater tendency to act on impulse. Verbal aggression—like calling someone a jerk—and physical aggression are ineffective ways of dealing with conflict. If your anger makes you aggressive, you have a major problem.

5. *When it disturbs work or relationships.* When your anger interferes with doing a good job or makes it hard for people to relate to you, then it becomes costly. It prevents concentration on your work and keeps you from being satisfied with your job. Anger often repels people and makes it difficult for them to like you.

Anger is always ugly, but it doesn't have to be bad. Learning to use its positive qualities will make your life a lot more productive.

TAKE ACTION

1. Practice saying to yourself: "Is my anger helping me or hurting me?"

2. Think of the last two times you got angry. Was your anger just? How do you know?

3. The next time you are angry, ask yourself: "How can I make my anger adaptive?"

4. Starting today, begin to "observe" (self-monitor) how you handle your anger. Use the "anger measurement box" (A.M.B.) to record your data. You will find just using the A.M.B. will lead to productive results. Completing the box will also help you pinpoint any anger problem area that you need to work out. For each anger problem area identified, use the recommended work-out(s).

Day	1	2	3	4	5	6	7	8	9	Work-outs Recommended
Frequency (How many times do you get angry each day?)										1,5,6,9, 11,14
Intensity (On the average, from 1–9, how physically aroused do you get each time you get angry; 9 is most intense. Use your heartbeat and breathing rate as data.)										4,5,9
Duration (On the average, how many minutes do you stay angry?)										6,7,12, 13,15
Instigates aggressiveness (How many times does your anger lead to aggression?)										4,5,6,9,10
Disturbs relationships (On the average, from 1–9, does your anger help or hurt relationships? 9 is most helpful.)										4,7,8, 9,11,12

THE BIGGEST MISTAKE PEOPLE MAKE
IN THIS WORK-OUT IS

to confuse needless anger with valid and just anger.

W O R K - O U T   N O T E S

_____

_____

_____

_____

_____

_____

_____

_____

_____

ANGER WORK-OUT #4

Avoiding the Anger Trap

PURPOSE

Anger is an escalating process. At its peak, our destructive self-statements and high level of anger arousal ignite an explosion. Almost all of us can remember a time when we took a swipe at someone—lover, child, sibling, parent—or if we didn't physically strike someone, we wounded our opponent by lashing out verbally.

When anger gets this hot, it is almost impossible to act or think productively because our thoughts, anger arousal, and behavior are escalating each other into a fury. We become trapped in our own anger. For most people, the fury subsides after they are emotionally spent, or when the other person outlasts them. Either way, the fallout is poisonous.

Anger Work-out #4 teaches a technique to help you avoid the anger trap. The technique is called *time-out* (*T.O.*), and it will immediately help you deescalate your anger before it becomes too intense.

Because intense anger leads to verbal and physical abuse for so many people, and because of its adverse physical effects, you are to begin using the time-out right away. That way, you can avoid the anger trap.

INFORMATION

Taking a Time-out (T.O.)

The strategy behind the time-out technique is to immediately isolate yourself from the anger-arousing situation. Taking this action will prevent your anger arousal from becoming intense, and at the same time help you reappraise the situation.

WORK-OUT NOTE

Although people have probably been using the time-out technique for thousands of years, it came into prominence as a behavior-modification technique in which a disruptive child would be removed from a situation (i.e., classroom, dinner table) for a designated period of time, and then would be allowed to return to the situation with the expectation that he would now act appropriately. The work-out process modifies the time-out technique so that you remove *yourself* from the situation rather than being removed by someone else. The emphasis is on managing yourself.

The T.O. is implemented when you say, out loud, to yourself, your wife, lover, kids, boss, parents:

"I'M BEGINNING TO FEEL ANGRY AND I WANT TO TAKE A TIME-OUT." THEN TAKE IT!

Saying this phrase *exactly* as it is written helps make the T.O. effective. Here's how.

I'm

An "I" statement. You begin by talking about yourself instead of name-calling or blaming.

Beginning to feel angry

You are talking about how you *feel*. This is a *direct* communication. There is nothing unclear about this statement.

I want to take a time-out

Besides making another "I" statement, you are also saying to the other person that you are going to do something other than explode. Your use of the word *want* will drum into your head the fact that you are making a choice to act in a productive way. DO NOT SAY *I NEED TO TAKE A TIME-OUT* because this implies that you are compelled to leave rather than wanting to leave. This is a Big Difference. Acknowledging that you are making a productive choice increases your confidence in dealing with anger. *Needing* to get away tells you: "You can't handle it."

When you take a time-out, here is what you do:

- You must leave the situation for one hour (no more and no less). This gives you *time* to cool down. Be sure to tell the person what a T.O. is and how it works. If another person is not involved, leave the situation anyhow. After you take your first step, the rest becomes easier.
- Do not drink or take drugs. Drinking and drugs will only make it worse.
- Do something constructively physical, such as walking, jogging, or cleaning the garage. Doing something physical will help discharge some of the angry tension in your body. Make sure that the activity is constructive.
- If you find yourself thinking about the situation that made you angry, say to your "self":
- I'M BEGINNING TO FEEL ANGRY AND I WANT TO TAKE A TIME-OUT.

In this way, you will be taking a *mental* time-out as well as a physical time-out. The merging of your productive self-statements and productive actions will cool down your anger arousal.

- After one hour, return to the situation if the person is still there, or phone him and ask if he would like to talk with you. If you both want to discuss the situation, tell him what it was that made you feel angry. Ask how he felt. You may want to talk about what it was like for each of you during the time-out. Share its effectiveness. This is the beginning of a productive anger dialogue.
- If one of you says, "I don't want to discuss this now," don't. Respect the other's wishes. If this makes you angry, take another time-out. The act of taking another time-out helps to strengthen your skill in using the T.O. effectively.

You will find some situations and subjects too hot to return to in one hour. In these cases, take a few hours, or even a few days. You must, however, return to the situation. Doing so will give you the opportunity to cope with it and build your confidence for handling future provocations. Equally important, when you return to the situation, you begin to build trust between those involved.

When intense anger and violence become integrated into a relationship, the trust factor drops significantly. Time-outs help you rebuild trust because every time you return from a time-out, you are confirming your commitment to the relationship.

Rebuilding that trust means investing your time and energy. Taking one or two time-outs does not mean everything is all right. It simply means the anger is under control. Develop your patience. Concentrate on identifying your anger and using your time-outs. They will work—if you take the step.

The creative time-out

What about the times when you get angry in a restaurant, at a party, at work, or while driving your car? How can you take a time-out in situations like these? The trick is to be creative and think of something that you can do that will prevent the situation from escalating. Although you can't leave a restaurant or party for an hour, you can go into a bathroom for ten minutes and wash your face. Or you might step outside for five minutes and get a breath of fresh air. Here are some examples of creative time-outs:

> *In a car:* Listen to three songs on the car radio before you
> continue your "discussion"; stop to get some gas and get out
> of your car for a stretch.
> *At work:* Take a ten-minute work break before getting back
> to the task at hand.
> *In a restaurant:* Order first, then talk.
> *Count to 50* before you respond.

All of these examples are based on the time-out strategy of interrupting your anger and can be used in confining situations.

As you become more skilled in taking regular time-outs, it will become easier for you to use creative time-outs.

Practice time-outs

Practice time-outs will help you take real time-outs. A practice time-out is the same as a real time-out except you are really *not* feeling angry, and they are only ten minutes long. It is just practice at saying the words and walking away. Tell your mate, "This is a practice time-out," then go on to say, "I'm beginning to feel angry and I want to take a time-out." The more you take practice time-outs, the *easier* it will be to take real time-outs.

WORK-OUT NOTE

It is important for you to take a time-out when you are becoming irritated because irritation can quickly become full-blown anger. Taking a time-out when you are irritated will also give you a head start in recognizing what provokes you. It is also easier to take a time-out when you are irritated than when you are angry. If you can't take a time-out at low levels of anger, it is doubtful that you will be able to take one when your anger becomes more intense.

TAKE ACTION

1. List three things you can do when you take a time-out. Knowing what to do now will make it easier to know what to do when you have to take a time-out.

   _____

   _____

   _____

2. List one creative time-out that you can use in each of the following situations (think of your own):

   In a restaurant:_____

   At work:_____

   In your car:_____

   At a social gathering:_____

3. During the next week, take three practice time-outs plus any when you are feeling angry, irritated, annoyed, or enraged.

4. Put time-out reminders in prominent places—on your desk, or on your night table—to help you remember that you have a response that will immediately stop anger from trapping you. The reminder should say: "I'm beginning to feel angry and I want to take a time-out."

THE BIGGEST MISTAKE PEOPLE MAKE
IN THIS WORK-OUT IS

that they say, "I'm beginning to feel angry and I want to take a time-out," but don't. Effective time-outs require action, not just productive self-statements. If you keep saying you want to take a time-out and don't, saying the phrase will in itself increase your anger because you will not be doing what you want. Time-outs are hard to do. Your first impulse will be to stay and resolve things, or at least get in the last word. But this only makes matters worse. Do not think that by walking away you are avoiding the problem or being unfair to other people. In fact, your taking a time-out will help them too. Do not be afraid that they will not be there when you return. This is part of the trust building. As you each follow through with your part in the time-out, your trust will grow. Although time-outs will be difficult for you initially, they will become easier with time and practice.

W O R K - O U T   N O T E S

_____

_____

_____

_____

_____

_____

_____

_____

_____

ANGER WORK-OUT #5
Getting Physical

PURPOSE

How does your body talk to you? What does it say when you're tired? Hungry? Sexy or happy?

Anger Work-out #5 will teach you how to hear your body talk so that you can use what it says to help you take better care of yourself, especially when you are angry.

WORK-OUT NOTE

What creates body talk (i.e., perhaps how you are appraising a situation) is not relevant in this work-out. The point is simply to be able to listen to it because it gives you another source of information that will help you take charge of yourself.

INFORMATION

Your Body Talks

Body talk means the signals from your body that tell you how it feels. When you can hear your body talk, you can become responsive to its needs. Failure to hear your body talk prevents you from taking care of it.

Sometimes your body talks to you in direct ways, as when you have a headache, a stomachache, sore muscles, or fatigue. Other times, it speaks only when provoked, as when you reach up and find that the muscles are sore.

In America, most people do not listen to their bodies talk. This is evidenced by the prevalence of such conditions as obesity, heart problems, and hypertension that could be controlled. A doctor may say, "You're not listening to your body. You've got to slow down." Unfortunately, these warnings are too often ignored.

The work-out process instructs you to listen to your body talk because your body knows when it is angry, or becoming so. If you listen to your body talk, you can use its signals as a cue that it's time to soothe your body's anger, and as a warning to find out what is causing the anger response.

When Your Body Talks Tensely

WORK-OUT NOTE

Although psychological and physical tension are interrelated, this work-out refers to physical tension only. Other work-outs will deal with psychological tension.

Tension is the *initial stage* in anger arousal. When we feel strung out, we are more easily provoked. Tense muscles, headaches, and tightness in the chest reduce our tolerance to cope effectively with daily provocations. If our tension level is high, we may treat a minor annoyance as though it were a catastrophe, with resultant waste of energy.

We all experience tension physically when we stay in the same position too long. Muscles benefit from movement and need the circulation of the blood that movement produces. Movement directly induces relaxation because muscles work in pairs, one group relaxing as the opposing group contracts. Bend your arm at the elbow and you'll get the point.

When muscles are tight and in static contraction for long periods, the circulation is impeded and there will be a build-up of fatigue, which may lead to muscle spasms (cramps). Holding a fist clenched for a while can significantly raise your blood pressure, and most dentists will warn you that continual tension of the jaw with teeth clenched tightly together is a common cause of tension headaches, as well as dental disorders. These are only some of the effects of sustained muscle tension.

Often our body tells us it's tense and we don't listen. Has your foot ever "fallen asleep"? Have you ever risen from a chair and noted soreness in your spine? And right now, some of you may be experiencing tension reading this book. Your shoulders may be stiff, legs cramped, and jaw clenched, causing fatigue and interfering with your ability to concentrate.

Intermittently, mild tension is not harmful, but prolonged tension does damage, wearing us out and draining physical and psychological resources that we need to deal effectively with daily provocations. Recognizing tension as a cue that anger may be brewing is essential.

WORK-OUT NOTE

An excellent example of the relationship between anger, tension, and your body is research that indicates that an inability to recognize and deal with anger is a major personality trait of people who experience migraine headaches. They fail to get the message even after it is hammered into their heads.

In order to hear your body say it's tense, you have to be aware of what it *feels* like in that condition. You can do this by *consciously* experiencing the difference between two polar states, tension and relaxation. A good method is to learn the tense-relax procedure that focuses on identifying the difference between feeling tension and relaxation in four major muscle groups:

- hands, forearms, and biceps
- head, face, throat, and shoulders
- thighs, buttocks, calves, and feet
- chest, stomach, and lower back

You can practice these procedures either lying down or in a chair with your hand supported. Each muscle group is tensed for approximately five seconds, then released for about twenty-five seconds. Once you have familiarized yourself with the procedures, you will be able to take action. Make sure you are in a comfortable position before you start.

Hands, Forearms, and Biceps

Clench your left fist tighter and tighter and be aware of the tension in your fist, your hand, and your forearm. Now relax. Feel the looseness in your hand and be aware of how it feels different from the tension. Do the same thing with your right fist.

Bend your elbows and tense your biceps, then relax and note the difference.

• Do each step at least once a day for one week.

Head, Neck, and Shoulders

These muscles are very important because from an emotional point of view, they are where many people store their tension.

Wrinkle your forehead as tight as you can. Feel the tension. Now relax and feel the difference.

Close your eyes as tight as you can. Feel the tension. Now relax and feel the difference.

Clench your jaw. Feel the tension in and around your mouth. Now relax and feel the difference.

Tighten your forehead, eyes, and jaw all together. Now relax and feel the difference. Enjoy the feeling of relaxation.

Move your head back as far as it can comfortably go. Be aware of the tension in your neck. Move your head around and note how the tension changes locations. Now relax and feel the difference.

Shrug your shoulders up hard, and press your head down between them. Now relax your shoulders and feel the difference.

• Do each step once a day for one week.

Thighs, Buttocks, Calves, and Feet

Tighten your buttocks and thighs by pressing down your head as hard as you can. Now relax and feel the difference.

Curl your toes downward. Note the tension in your calves. Now relax and feel the difference.

Force your toes upward. Note the tension in your shins. Now relax and feel the difference.

Note how your legs feel.

• Do each step at least once a day for one week.

Chest, Stomach, and Lower Back

Take a deep breath, hold it and feel the tension. Then exhale and feel your chest relax. Note how the tension affects your breathing.

Breathe deeply and slowly for a minute and feel the tension leaving your body.

Tighten your stomach muscles. Now relax and feel the difference.

Tighten your back but do not strain it. Feel the tension in your lower back. Now relax and feel the difference.

- Do each step at least once a day for one week.

WORK-OUT NOTE

Many therapists call this procedure progressive relaxation and use it as a way to teach relaxation. The work-out process uses the term tense-relax to emphasize that the chief concern here is to be able to *identify tension,* not to learn to relax. In a later work-out (#9) you will be taught what to do to develop a relaxation response, and how and when to use it. However, if you can't identify *when* you are tense, not only can you not reap the full benefits of a relaxation response, your ability to know *what* is making you angry will be impaired.

LOOK AT YOUR HANDS AND OTHERS' SEVERAL TIMES A DAY TO SEE WHEN TENSION IS PRESENT AND FISTS ARE FORMING.

When Your Body Yells

If you ignore your body when it tells you it is tense, chances are, it will soon yell at you because it wants you to know that something is wrong. It's hard to believe, but even when most people's bodies are yelling at them, they still don't listen. Even when your body is breathing hard, perspiring, and jacking up its blood pressure, you still ignore it. At this point, your body gets so angry that it may attack your heart!

If you think this doesn't happen to you, think again. Remember the last time you were in a heated argument with your lover, or angry about something at work. Despite the fact that your body was yelling at you, you probably continued arguing or being very upset.

It's bad enough when you don't hear your body say it's tense, but it's worse when you ignore its yelling because you end up yelling too (if not at others, at yourself). You say things that you later regret and you act impulsively. When you are acting like this, your body is in a state of anger arousal, and not recognizing it can be fatal.

The best way to know when your body is experiencing this state is to develop a sensitivity to your different levels of physical arousal, paying particular attention to those bodily or somatic functions that are disturbed when your body experiences anger arousal. These include your heart rate, perspiration rate, respiration rate, and muscular tension. They also include any other changes that are unique to you. All these somatic functions are different when you are physically aroused, not aroused at all, or anger aroused. The better you become at noticing the differences among these physical states, the faster you can use anger arousal as a cue that your body is yelling at you. Taking action will help you be sensitive to your body's physical changes.

W O R K - O U T   N O T E

Research indicates that you can learn to monitor the somatic changes your body undergoes when it's angry by simply practicing awareness of them. They are all correlated. This means that if your heart is beating faster than usual, your blood pressure and respiratory rate are increasing also. The concurrence of these changes facilitates awareness of them.

PAY ATTENTION TO THE PALMS OF YOUR HANDS. WHEN THEY ARE WET, YOU KNOW YOUR RESPIRATION RATE IS UP. ANGER MAY BE SNEAKING UP ON YOU.

PAY ATTENTION TO HOW MOIST YOUR MOUTH IS. IF IT'S DRY, YOU MAY BE STEAMING.

Talking Back

When your body talks, not only do you need to listen, you need to respond. Here are some ways to talk back to your body.

When your body says it's tense (aim to break the tension):

- The ten-second massage. Whether it's a stiff neck, a stiff shoulder, or a headache, ten seconds of rubbing will reduce tension and make you feel better.
- Relax it away. If you do not have a relaxation response (Work-out #9 will give you one), taking two or three slow, deep breaths will do the trick.
- Change your posture. Whether you're sitting or standing, changing the position of your body will break the lock. This is great for when you are driving in heavy traffic after a hard day's work, or sitting at your desk doing an important task. Just move a little in your seat.
- Reaching out. Extending your arms and legs gets the crinks out and the circulation moving. Reaching out gets you the help you need.
- Give yourself a wink. Close your eyes for less than a minute and shut out the pressure. When you open your eyes, you may see things differently. (Of course, this is not recommended while driving!)

When your body yells (aim to decrease your breathing, heart, and respiration rates and blood pressure):

- Talk more slowly. Did you ever hear anybody yell slowly, not including cheerleaders?
- Breathe longer and more deeply. This helps you get rid of your hot air.
- Get yourself a drink of water. This will literally help you cool off. Drinks with caffeine may stimulate the fight-flight response and increase the arousal you want to slow down.
- If you are standing, sit down. Nobody ever has a peace talk standing up. Sitting down helps quash your anger arousal and makes you more comfortable.
- If you are sitting down, lean back. When you're yelling, leaning forward is part of the fighting posture. Remember, "lean back and enjoy the show" is *less exciting* than sitting on the edge of your chair.
- Keep your hands at your sides. Shaking your fists and waving your arms speeds up your circulation. Keeping your hands at your sides prevents you from shaking things up or striking out.
- Quiet yourself. You're bound to get angry if someone tells you to shut up, so you're better off saying it to yourself. Silence is golden in these situations.

As you begin to pay more and more attention to what your body says, you will be able to give it what it needs. It will then be much happier and have less reason to yell at you.

TAKE ACTION

1. Begin to pay attention to your body talk and list the ways that it talks (the physical signals it sends off) when:

   You are tired:_____

   You are stressed:_____

   You are anxious:_____

   You are happy:_____

2. Practice the tense-relax exercise once a day for a week.

3. During the next week, begin to note your body's feelings when you are physically aroused and not physically aroused, paying particular attention to your heart rate, breathing rate, and muscular tension. This will help you know when your body is talking loudly to you.

   Begin to pay particular attention to *when* you are angry. List all the somatic disturbances you experienced, but pay particular attention to your heart rate and breathing rate.

   _____   _____

   _____   _____

   _____   _____

4. Compare your heart rate and breathing rate (and comfort) when you are angry to when you are generally physically aroused, and not aroused at all. (You will note that your heart rate and breathing rates are significantly faster when you are experiencing anger arousal.)

   When you are angry, which somatic disturbances do you notice first?

   _____

   This is your somatic key cue that your body is yelling.

5. List some things you can do when your body talks tensely.

   _____

   _____

   _____

6. List some things you can do that will slow your body down when it yells.

   _____

   _____

   _____

THE BIGGEST MISTAKE PEOPLE MAKE
IN THIS WORK-OUT IS

to fail to take action. As a result, they continue to ignore their body's talk, leaving their body no option but to yell at them more and more. Their body usually ends up yelling at the top of its lungs.

W O R K - O U T   N O T E S

_____

_____

_____

_____

_____

_____

_____

_____

_____

_____

ANGER WORK-OUT #6

Head Tripping or How to Outthink Anger

Recommended for:
1. People who are chronically angry
2. People who don't want to be neurotic
3. People who want to reduce destructive anger
4. People who don't think they can handle a situation
5. People who don't help themselves when they're angry
6. People who want to manage themselves
7. People who want to think clearly

PURPOSE

Among the many ways that our thoughts influence how we feel is through the things we say to ourselves. Our internal conversations, private speech, thought talk, or self-statements are the mechanisms that allow us to bring to life the appraisals we make and the expectations we have. The statements that we make to ourselves precede, accompany, or follow the things we feel.

In an anger situation, self-statements play an important part in defining and shaping our emotions. For example: "I'm going to tell that son of a bitch to shove it. I'm not going to take this crap anymore." "Jeez, she's a real pain in the ass. I'm going to fix her good." Self-statements such as these add fuel to the fire and prolong anger after an incident is over.

Anger Work-out #6 makes use of a basic premise of the work-out process: The self-statements we make in anger situations are habitual and destructive. Some people "automatically" see themselves as victims of malice, while some habitually magnify the danger. Others expect the world to cave in. But just as our self-statements can stir up and prolong our anger, they can also be used to regulate and control it.

Anger Work-out #6 will help you identify and countermand your counterproductive self-statements so that you can replace them with more realistic and functional ones. As this process occurs, you gain greater control of your anger, enabling you to wipe out needless anger and begin to direct just anger productively.

INFORMATION

Thinking Up Anger

Many of the self-statements you make when you are angry are created by a distorted thinking style. A distorted thinking style causes you to misinterpret the reality of the situation and makes you prone to anger distortions—self-statements that provoke your anger. These self-statements are bound to create needless and unjust anger because they are not based on an accurate interpretation of the situation.

Continually using the same distorted thinking style develops the habit of using the same self-statements every time you are angry and, in the process, reinforces the distorted thinking style that started it. Becoming aware of the distorted thinking styles you use will make it easier for you to recognize your anger distortions so that you can combat them.

W O R K - O U T   N O T E

A matter of clarification: Your anger may be provoked in a just manner with no cognitive distortions present, such as when someone is abusing you. However, once you are angry, cognitive distortions are quick to surface. For example: "He's saying these things because he doesn't love me," whereas he is saying these things because he is retaliating for something unkind said to him moments earlier. In contrast, distorted thinking styles initiate the anger rather than appear *after* you are angry. These distorted thinking styles create anger distortions—self-statements that provoke your anger.

There are four different types of distorted thinking that will make you angry.

Destructive labeling

One of the most potent distorted thinking styles is destructive labeling, an extreme form of overgeneralization. When you use destructive labeling, you generalize one or two qualities into a negative global judgment. For example, calling your spouse an S.O.B., or your boss a jerk, presents them in a totally negative way.

Someone may in fact have violated your trust, and you are absolutely just to resent what that person did. But by making the other person totally negative, you become inappropriately indignant and morally superior: They are wrong—you are right—when, in fact, you are both "right" and "wrong." Destructive labeling creates and perpetuates anger because it forces you to focus on the "negative" characteristics that you find provoking in another person. Continually thinking about these characteristics festers up your anger, making it more and more intense until an anger feedback loop makes it needless and unjust.

Mind reading

When you mind-read, you invent motives and make assumptions that explain to your satisfaction why the other person did what he or she did. These assumptions are frequently erroneous because they do not describe the *actual* thoughts and perceptions that motivate the other person. Your anger prevents you from thinking about what you are saying to yourself.

Some of the typical "anger explanations" that we use to explain someone's objectionable behavior include:

He doesn't care about me.
She really wanted to hurt me.

Mind reading, then, makes us angry because we think that the other person "thinks/feels that way."

WORK-OUT NOTE

Some therapists believe that mind reading is based on a process called projection. You imagine that people feel the same way you do and react to things the same way you do. Therefore, you don't watch or listen closely enough to notice that they are actually different. If you get angry when your spouse is late, you assume that if you are late, she will get angry with you. If she doesn't greet you with a hug and a kiss when you are ten minutes late, you assume that she is angry at you instead of thinking, "She doesn't like to kiss in public," or "She doesn't kiss me all the time anyway." You then get angry at her for being angry at you. Whether or not projection is the underlying process for mind reading does not change the fact that when we do mind-read, the results can be disastrous.

Magnification

Magnification is exaggerating the significance of a negative event. The process of magnifying distorts your thoughts by making everything seem worse than it really is. You are actually making a mountain out of a molehill. Magnification frequently occurs when you are slightly irritated; perhaps you are stuck in traffic when you have an important meeting, or perhaps someone forgets to give you an important message. You begin to tell yourself, "This is terrible. I'm missing my big opportunity. I can't believe this is happening to me."

Magnification creates anger because it *intensifies* and increases the *duration* of your emotional reaction way out of proportion. Before you know it, your anger is full-blown—and for what purpose?

Imperatives

With this type of distorted thinking, you have a list of inflexible rules about how you and other people should act. When you find other people's actions are not to your liking, you tell yourself they "shouldn't" do that, or they "should have" done something they failed to do. Cue words indicating the presence of this distortion are *should, ought,* or *must.*

This distorted thinking style creates anger because it implies that we are entitled to get what we want in a specific situation, or that people should be the way we want them to be. Consequently, when our imperatives are violated, we perceive that an injustice has taken place, causing us to feel anger.

Violating our own self-requirements also creates self-anger because we perceive the violation as failure. In reality, the violation reflects the fact that we did not meet our unrealistically high expectations, a trait of the chronically angry person. Some of the most common and unreasonable expectations are:

I should be totally self-reliant.
I should assert myself and at the same time never hurt anyone else.
I should never be angry with my parents.
I should never be angry with my kids.
I should always love the same person.

As you become more familiar with your "angry thoughts" you may find that you have a favorite anger distortion, or that you tend to use all of them. One thought to remember is that by using any or all of the anger distortions, you create much of your own anger needlessly and perpetuate it endlessly.

How Your Thoughts Think

After you are able to identify your distorted thinking, you are ready to home in on specific self-statements that create and perpetuate your anger.

Because these thoughts come so quickly, and because they seem to occur without any prior reasoning or reflection, they are called *automatic thoughts.*

Hearing your automatic thoughts is important for three reasons. First, the process of hearing them gives you practice in paying attention to the specific self-statements you are making when you are angry. Second, your counterproductive automatic thoughts will in themselves be a *cue* that you need to talk to yourself differently—in a way that helps you manage your anger, rather than promote it. And third, censoring your counterproductive automatic thoughts will help you avoid distorted thinking styles that create needless anger and other distressful emotions.

Automatic thoughts have the following characteristics:

They are private. Most people talk to themselves differently from the way they talk to others. When we talk to others, we tend to describe our life events in a rational manner. But when we talk to ourselves, we are frequently irrational and use horrifying overgeneralizations such as "I'm a failure. Nobody will ever love me."

They are almost always believed by us. Despite their irrationality, automatic thoughts are unquestioningly accepted. They seem plausible because they are hardly noticed. We don't question them or challenge them, nor are their implications logically analyzed.

They are discrete and specific messages. They give us a direct and distinct message about some event, such as "He doesn't love me."

They usually appear in brief form. Automatic thoughts are frequently abbreviated to one word, or a transient visual image. For example, a rising executive may say, "Zip," to tell himself that he will be left with no job after a company merger. A woman who envisions her husband talking to an attractive lady may use the image to tell herself her husband doesn't love her anymore, or that he is having an affair.

They are learned. Since we were born, people have been telling us what to think. Our family, friends, teachers, and even the media condition us to appraise events in specific ways.

They tend to be catastrophic. Automatic thoughts tend to act as cues for other thoughts. One depressing thought may trigger a whole chain of depressing thoughts.

They are hard to turn off. Because automatic thoughts go unnoticed, they seem to come and go as they wish.

Here is an example of an automatic thought that typically happens when your lover is expressing anger at you.

Automatic thought: "That's it."
Really means: "I can't stand him. I want a divorce. He is so inconsiderate. Our marriage is over. How will I support myself? What about the kids?"

A good way to become aware of how your automatic thoughts affect you is to keep a thought diary. Make an entry every time you experience distressful feelings and emotions—especially anger—and write down what you tell yourself. You will be amazed at how your distressful feelings coincide with your counterproductive automatic thoughts.

Talking Yourself Sane

Anger distortions are mental punches that you inflict on your "self." Their end result is to knock you senseless.

The most effective means to combat your anger distortions is to "mentally fight back" and the technique to use is counterpunching. Counterpunching with the mind is identical to counterpunching in a fight. It is automatically matching every distorted statement that you make with a rational comeback—a self-statement that helps you accurately appraise the given situation.

To use this technique effectively, counterpunch as soon as you are beginning to feel angry, or when you are angry. At these times, ask yourself the question:

WHAT AM I TELLING MYSELF ABOUT THIS SITUATION?

Your answer will make you aware of the self-statements you are saying, the distorted thinking style you are using, and what counterpunch to use. If a distorted thinking style is absent, it's a signal that your anger is probably just.

Listed below are effective counterpunch statements that reflect the rational correlatives to each of the four distorted thinking styles that provoke and perpetuate anger. Remembering these counterpunches and grasping the concepts they reflect will help you "keep things in perspective," thus preventing you from punishing yourself with needless and destructive anger. Evaluation of a situation becomes easier and the best actions to be taken are more readily determined. There are two other benefits of counterpunching. First, it helps you put past anger in perspective. You can zero in on the past angers that were needless or unjust. In many instances, correcting past distortions will free you from the effects of past anger that interfere with your present life (using counterpunching this way gives you a head start for doing Anger Work-out #16). Counterpunching will also improve the quality of your relationships because you will be cutting down on needless and unjust anger that you direct to others.

READ THE COUNTERPUNCHES ALOUD. AFTER YOU KNOW THE CONCEPTS THEY REFLECT, PUT THE COUNTERPUNCHES INTO YOUR OWN WORDS.

Distortion in Action: *Destructive Labeling*	*Counterpunch Examples*
You tell yourself that the person is terrible because of a specific thing he or she did.	Say it to yourself: Be specific. This isn't always true.

Concept for Counterpunching Destructive Labeling

Destructive labels are inaccurate because they describe the whole picture on the basis of one or two incidents. They are based on *minimum cognitive engagement*. Limit your observations to a specific case and gather as much data as you can to get a better view of the whole picture.

Distortion in Action: *Mind Reading*	*Counterpunch Examples*
You tell yourself what other people are thinking and feeling without their saying so.	Say to yourself: How do I know? Check it out.

Concept for Counterpunching Mind Reading

Mind reading is making inferences about how people feel and think. Because it is impossible for you to ever know exactly what another is thinking or feeling, you are better off either believing them or validating your assumptions by asking them. Do not make snap judgments about someone else's thoughts or actions without appropriate evidence.

Distortion in Action: Imperatives	Counterpunch Example
You get angry at people who violate your list of rules. You also feel guilty and angry if you violate the rules.	Say to yourself: Be flexible. They can do it differently.

Concept for Counterpunching Imperatives

Review and question your personal rules and expectations. Be on guard for words like *should, ought,* and *must.* When your thinking is flexible, you don't use these words because you know there are always exceptions and special circumstances. Getting angry when people don't act according to your personal rules and values is valid, but remember that they are not you. Your rules may work for you but not for others. Recognize that people are different. You are entitled to your opinion, but allow for differences of opinion.

Distortion in Action: Magnification	Counterpunch Example
You tell yourself: "This is terrible, a disaster. I can't take it."	Say to yourself: No need to magnify. Don't make it worse than it is. I can cope. What are the realistic odds of this really screwing things up—90 percent? .05 percent? 30 percent? Check out the reality of the situation.

Concept for Counterpunching Magnification

Magnification takes things out of perspective and intensifies your anger arousal. Stop using words like *terrible, awful, disgusting, horrendous.* In particular, banish the phrase "I can't stand it." You can stand it, because human beings can withstand severe psychological blows or physical pain. You can get used to and cope with almost anything.

You can improve your skill at counterpunching by using the Three Column Technique. This entails writing down anger experiences that are current in your mind. Then write down thoughts you had in the anger situation and check for any cognitive distortions. Next rewrite the statement without the distortion; in this way, you get practice for correcting your thinking and for recognizing the faulty logic you used. This makes counterpunching easier to use in actual situations.

WORK-OUT NOTE

People who are good counterpunchers have excellent staying power. They do not counterpunch just once or twice. They keep punching until they knock the anger distortion clear out of their minds. This is the trick to counterpunching—you must keep it up. Think of yourself as Rocky and go the distance; otherwise the anger distortion will get up off its feet and bang you around some more. Remember, your anger distortions have been winning for years. Eventually, they will disappear and you will be left with productive ways of appraising a situation.

Thinking Through Anger

Many times you will be angry and there will be no anger distortions. Your anger is valid and just. There will also be many times when you know you will soon be confronting a situation that could be anger arousing. In these situations, you can manage your anger by using your self-statements as self-instructions—specific statements that tell you what to do when you are getting angry or about to confront a provocation. Here are some examples of effective "anger-management statements" that you may use, but it is also a good idea to develop your own:

I can work out a plan to handle this.
Remember, stick to the issues and don't take it personally.
Don't yell.
Take a deep breath.
Listen to what they say.

Using self-statements like this is effective because they control your anger arousal, guide your behavior in a productive direction, prevent you from getting sidetracked, and give you confidence that you can cope with provocation.

As you continue to work out, you will begin to replace your old "automatic" counterproductive thoughts with productive self-statements. The success you experience will reinforce their continual use. Inevitably, it will become second nature to use them. When this happens, it becomes easier to outthink anger because your head is no longer tripping you up.

TAKE ACTION

1. Right now, sit back and just listen to yourself talk. Make believe you are listening in on someone's telephone conversation.
   Notice how quickly you talk and how one or two words is really the equivalent of several sentences. Do this for two or three minutes.

2. Keep a thought diary for three days. Use the following format to get started. At the end of the day reread your thoughts. Your distortions will jump out.

Emotion	Automatic Thought
_____	_____
_____	_____
_____	_____

3. Practice counterpunching concepts by completing the following sentences with your own words:

   If I magnify, I will tell myself_____

   If I destructively label, I will tell myself_____

   If I make imperatives, I will tell myself_____

   If I mind-read, I will tell myself_____

   If I say it's not fair, I will tell myself_____

4. Use the Three Column Technique for a recent anger situation(s).

   Anger situation_____

A	B	C
Original thought	Distortion	Rewritten statement without distortion
_____	_____	_____

5. Write two anger-management statements that you can use the next time you confront a provocation. (Make sure your statements are specific—"Take a deep breath" instead of "Relax.")

   _____

   _____

THE BIGGEST MISTAKE PEOPLE MAKE
IN THIS WORK-OUT IS

that they don't recognize and acknowledge their distorted thinking and therefore cannot combat destructive self-statements. The best way to avoid this is to write down your thoughts in detail. This is a nuisance at first, but the more you write, the more your anger distortions can surface, increasing your chances to outthink them.

W O R K - O U T   N O T E S

_____

_____

_____

_____

_____

_____

_____

_____

_____

_____

_____

ANGER WORK-OUT #7

Feeling Good and Angry

> *Recommended for:*
> 1. *People who have difficulty feeling their anger*
> 2. *People who have trouble talking about their feelings*
> 3. *People who are unsure of their feelings*
> 4. *People who feel guilty about their feelings*
> 5. *People who want to feel better*

PURPOSE

Many people have difficulty handling feelings, which causes emotional distress for them and others. This is especially true for anger. For most of us, it's too hot to handle. That's why it's usually squelched or runs ablaze. Anger Work-out #7 begins the process of helping you learn how to handle your feelings. When you can handle your feelings, it becomes easier to work out your anger. It also becomes easier to help other people work out their anger.

INFORMATION

The Nature of Feelings

In their purest form, feelings represent the sensations we experience by touch. We assume that if we touch something, we know how it feels. In this context, physical touch helps us learn "feelings." For example, we can learn how cold feels by touching an ice cube, or how lukewarm feels by dipping a hand in tepid water. We learn the "feel" of velvet by stroking it.

We touch thousands of things every day, yet it would be hard for you right now to get a good "feel" for each and every thing. For instance, what does your kitchen table feel like? Can you get a good feel for its texture? Can you remember the feel of the fabric of yesterday's clothes? What does your lover's hand feel like?

These sensations often escape us, even when we are directly experiencing them. At the dinner table we are aware of the taste of food rather then being aware of how the table and chair feel. Sometimes, we're not even aware of our hand resting on somebody else's. Just because we're touching does not mean we're feeling.

FEELING WHAT YOU TOUCH WILL INCREASE YOUR SENSITIVITY.

Another way that we touch (and are touched by others) is through "psychological touches." A psychological touch occurs when an experience *affects* us, when it impresses us and changes our *subjective* experience of the world. Falling in love is being psychologically touched. So is being angry. Psychological touches differ from physical touches in that they do not necessarily involve making physical contact, although physical sensations are often the reference for psychological feelings. A shock from touching an electric wire or numbness of the mouth after a novocaine injection becomes a reference point for understanding the feelings of someone who says, "I'm shocked," or "I'm numb." When we are psychologically touched, we experience a feeling.

Unlike physical touch, psychological touch is much more subjective because there is no direct physical and objective reference point, only your own perception. This subjective viewpoint is the basis for the nature of your feelings.

Nobody can tell you what you are feeling. Nor can anybody tell you why you feel a particular way. But people frequently try to do just that.

"You feel so indifferent to me."
"You're angry at me because I didn't call."

Other times, people tell you that they don't know how you feel.

"I never know what you're feeling. You never tell me how you feel."

And many times people wish they knew what you were feeling.

"Gee, I wonder how she really feels about me."

These observations point up one of the major purposes for expressing feelings: They communicate to others the value that an experience has for us. That is, how we are *affected* by what they do or say. How we are touched. But despite the significant role that feelings play in our lives, we do not always recognize them, let alone express them. Individuals have their own reasons for not recognizing and expressing their feelings, but there are general reasons.

For one thing, many of us are taught that feelings are unimportant, unpredictable, irrational, unfair, and potentially explosive, as with anger. If we exhibit angry feelings, we are seen as losing control. Men are taught that showing "sensitive" feelings is a sign of weakness and is not macho. Women are told that it's all right to express feelings, but many still hide them. It is very difficult to express and acknowledge our feelings when we are given so many messages to the contrary.

We also fail to acknowledge our feelings from fear of having to deal with consequences. This is especially true with anger because the emotion of anger touches us psychologically, leading to feelings that are uncomfortable—hurt, rejection, shame, embarrassment, hate, and even love. These feelings are difficult to cope with because their subjective nature is distressful. Stuffing them becomes safer. Similarly, many people do not acknowledge love because dealing with feelings of intimacy may be overwhelming. Feelings frighten us. Part of working out anger is being able to handle the feelings that our emotional anger creates.

We also suppress our feelings because we don't want to deal with another person's response to them. Not telling a person that we are angry at him, or that we don't like him, or that we do like him saves us from dealing with *his* feelings of anger, grief, or love.

Sometimes we choose not to express or acknowledge our feelings because they make us vulnerable to hurt. In fact, the fear of being rejected is perhaps the major reason why we hesitate to express our feelings. These concerns are real and make a valid point: After we are aware of our feelings, it is our *choice* whether and how we express them.

Feeling Awareness

Before we can learn to handle our feelings, we have to acknowledge them. Some feelings are easier to acknowledge than others. For example, it is a lot easier to acknowledge that we are feeling happy than that we are feeling sad. Positive feelings are pleasant. Negative feelings may hurt us.

Many people confuse feelings with *thinking or observation.*

"I feel it wasn't right that you didn't call me."
"I feel that you are lying to me."
"I feel you don't love me."

"I feel it wasn't right." How can that be? How can we *feel* "It wasn't right"? Right is not a feeling. It is an evaluative *thought.* We frequently express our feelings as thoughts because we don't know exactly how to describe them *when* we experience them. Feelings expressed through thoughts are known as *I-feel-thinking statements* rather than *I-feel-emotion statements.* A good rule for whether you are making an I-feel-thinking statement is to replace "I feel" with "I think." If it makes sense, then it is probably a thinking statement rather than a feeling-emotion statement (i.e., "I think it wasn't right that you didn't call me" makes sense). The previous I-feel-thinking statements can be changed to I-feel-emotion statements:

"I feel it was not right that you didn't call me" becomes "I feel hurt that you didn't call me."
"I feel you are lying to me" becomes "I feel frustrated that you are lying to me."
"I feel that you don't love me" becomes "I feel sad that you don't love me."

Recognizing I-feel-thinking statements is important because you can use them as a *cue* to indicate that you are having difficulty in expressing feelings. When you are able to change I-feel-thinking statements into I-feel-emotion statements, you communicate more accurately to your "self" and others what you are experiencing. Knowing what you are experiencing allows you to get a handle on your feelings.

Given all these obstacles and problems, why should you want to be more aware of your feelings? You've already heard part of the answer. Feelings provide you with important information about yourself and your judgment of whatever situation you are in. And work-out experts agree that people who make decisions using both *thinking* and *feeling* responses are more likely to be happier with their results.

Being aware of your feelings will also prevent stress from becoming distress. Feelings can cause stress, but that stress can be reduced by acknowledging and expressing those feelings. If you break up with your lover, or a loved one dies, it is stressful to deal with the feelings of hurt that you may feel. If you choose to deny the hurt, the stress becomes distress. Expressing the feelings of hurt and love will free you to move on to the next phase of your life.

Another important reason to be aware of your feelings and to be able to express them is that it fosters psychological intimacy. When you acknowledge how you feel, you are sharing your very own perceptions of the world with someone else. In a sense, you are inviting a person into your world. There is absolutely no doubt that people who share feelings have a better chance for having a productive relationship.

In addition, being aware of feelings and expressing them allows you to be real, to be yourself. By being yourself, you don't communicate confusing messages that inhibit trust.

What can you do to become more aware of your feelings and express them so they reflect what you experience? One thing is to pay attention to the physical sensations that each feeling stirs in you. You may have already begun to identify the physical signs of anger, and you may be pretty good at recognizing them now. Other feelings have physical signs too. When you become sensitive to the physical sensations of each feeling, it becomes easier to differentiate your feelings from one another. This helps you to know what you are feeling. Keeping a feeling diary will help too because it forces you to monitor your feelings. As you use your diary, you increase your awareness of how and what you feel each day.

Expressing Feelings

After becoming aware of your feelings, the next step is learning to (and how you) express them.

In intimate relationships, we almost always express our feelings. Sometimes we do it directly, but at other times we do it indirectly—by the tone of our voice, our body posture, eye contact, or facial expression. Many times, especially with anger, we hide our feelings by saying something that is very different from what we really feel. This leads to confusion, since what we say is contradicted by our behavior, voice, or gestures. Hiding our feelings may protect us, but when there is confusion in a relationship, there is little chance for trust. Having a healthy intimate relationship and being who we are depends on expressing our feelings clearly.

There is one more important point to make about your feelings. Although you have the right to express your feelings, you do not have the right to expect other people to change because of the way you feel. The fact is, they may choose not to change, even after you have expressed that you feel bad about something they are doing. You can't force someone to change. If your lover does decide to change her behavior, it is because she sees who you are and because she cares about how you feel. In short, you need to trust her goodwill toward you. If your trust is low, begin to build it up by acknowledging your feelings and expressing them directly. Remember, where feelings aren't expressed clearly, a healthy, intimate relationship is impossible.

TAKE ACTION

1. Feel some things that are rough, smooth, and warm.

2. Read each of the following "feeling" words out *loud* three or four times. Change the tone of your voice each time, making sure you say each word softly and loudly. As you read each word, note the sensations that each feeling stirs up in you and how they differ. See if you get a feeling for some words but not others.

hurt	depressed	tense	scared
happy	lonely	frightened	loving
content	anxious	enthusiastic	weak

3. Keep a feeling diary for at least one week, the longer the better.

   ### *Feelings I Had Today*

Monday	I felt _____
Tuesday	I felt _____
Wednesday	I felt _____
Thursday	I felt _____
Friday	I felt _____
Saturday	I felt _____
Sunday	I felt _____

4. Think of how you can express each of the following feelings so that your lover knows you are experiencing them:

happiness	love
sadness	anger
fear	enthusiasm

   Think about how your lover expresses these feelings to you.

5. During the next week, use an I-feel-emotion statement toward your lover three times a day. Then think about why you express some feelings and not others.

THE BIGGEST MISTAKE PEOPLE MAKE
IN THIS WORK-OUT IS

that they *think* they are "wrong" to feel a certain way. Feelings are not right or wrong. They are just feelings.

W O R K - O U T   N O T E S

_____

_____

_____

_____

_____

_____

_____

_____

_____

_____

ANGER WORK-OUT #8
P.S. No More B.S.!

Recommended for:
1. *People who yell and scream*
2. *People who experience migraine headaches*
3. *People who have ulcers*
4. *People who are depressed*
5. *People who are obese*
6. *People who are substance abusers*
7. *People who have poor personal relationships*
8. *People who have low self-esteem*
9. *People who want to communicate productively*

PURPOSE

Failure to express anger productively can lead to violence and other destructive behaviors such as substance abuse, obesity, ulcers, migraine headaches, and broken hearts. Anger Work-out #8 will teach you how to develop a productive anger style, and what to do when productive anger expression is sabotaged by others.

INFORMATION

The Three Anger Styles

The three styles of anger expression are called *stuffing, escalating,* and *directing.* Stuffing and escalating always work against you.

WORK-OUT NOTE

People adapt these anger styles partly because they have been "taught" that this is how to express anger and/or because their behavior has been reinforced in some way. Recall the concepts of modeling and operant learning.

Stuffing

When you stuff your anger, you "move away" from directly confronting the person (or situation) that is provoking the anger. The reason for stuffing varies with the individual, but some of the more common reasons are fear of hurting another person, thinking it is inappropriate to be angry or to be angry at a particular person, fear of being rejected, and/or not being able to cope with the emotional impact of interpersonal conflict. Not having to deal with these consequences reinforces the stuffing style. In its extreme emotional form, stuffing reflects the instinctual flight response.

In its simplest form, stuffing is easy to recognize. It begins typically with an "I statement" and is followed by some words that deny that you are feeling angry, or deny your right to be angry. Stuffing is also used when you acknowledge that you are angry and withdraw from the situation without saying you are angry. Here are some examples:

"I'm not angry or upset."
"He really doesn't mean to upset me."
"I really shouldn't be angry at him."
"I better not tell him I'm angry."
"I won't call her."

Walking away when you are boiling inside, but trying not to show it.

Stuffing is a counterproductive anger style because:

Stuffed anger is expressed anyhow. It may be disguised as sarcasm, intentionally forgetting to do something for the person at a later date, holding back your love, or avoiding the person in the future. But it is expressed nonetheless. Stuffed anger is sometimes hard to recognize (for both the stuffer and the person involved) because the stuffers deny that they are angry, even when confronted. Their actions, however, betray them.

There are adverse health effects. Stuffing anger results in many physical and mental ills such as ulcers, migraine headaches, obesity, and depression.

The provocation continues. When you stuff your anger, you have no opportunity to confront the provocation productively and work out your anger. The provocation continues, the stuffing continues, and the harmful effects continue too.

Your relationship suffers. Stuffing anger is incompatible with a productive relationship. Denying you are angry, or withdrawing from your lover, does not give the two of you the chance to work out the "problem." Instead, tension builds until there is an explosion. This is when you may hear "Why didn't you say something before?"

Escalating

Escalating is much easier to identify than stuffing. "Escalators" almost always begin their sentences with "You!" They frequently ask accusatory questions: "Why did you do that?" They blame: "You made me angry. . . . It's your fault." And they shame: "You bitch . . . you asshole." Their means of expression is frequently ranting and raving. If you escalate your anger, you are putting yourself in a paradoxical situation: Your attempt to control the situation makes things worse. In its extreme emotional form, escalating reflects the instinctual fight response. Escalating is a counterproductive anger style because:

The constant and intense anger arousal can kill you. Frequent and intense anger arousal makes you prone to heart attacks.

Constant escalating destroys your relationships and will bring violence into them. A major reason for divorce is frequent fighting outbursts.

Escalators may "get their way" but only in the short run. Your opponents may give in to avoid your fury, but they will get back at you somehow, even in disguised fashion.

Directing

Directing your anger is a productive anger style because you clearly and appropriately express to the provoking person that you are angry at him. Completing the following sentences with a concise statement will help you direct your anger.

I FEEL ANGRY_____

I WOULD LIKE_____

Here is an example:

I feel angry that you lied to me.
I would like you to be honest with me.

People who express their anger directly get their message across, feel more intimate, communicate better, and generally feel as though they have made contact in a personal way.

By now you probably realize that at various times you have either stuffed, escalated, or directed your anger. The more aware you become of how you express your anger, the more control you will have over dealing with it.

WHEN YOU DIRECT YOUR ANGER, MAKE SURE YOUR VOICE LEVEL IS NOT TOO LOUD AND THAT YOU HAVE GOOD EYE CONTACT.

De-fense, *De*-fense, *De*-fense

Many times your productive anger expression is sabotaged by the target of your anger, who responds either by ignoring your message or by getting angry and defensive. This typically leads to frustration and anger of your own, which quickly escalates the situation, thus justifying the other person's right to ignore you. A good way to prevent this destructive pattern is to learn how to overcome the "blocking gambits" that people use.

A blocking gambit is a style of communication that one may use to avoid confronting anger, dealing with distress, or acknowledging the undesired behavior that provokes you.

Some of the most troublesome blocking gambits that you will encounter include:

Laughing it off. Your anger is responded to with a joke or some other attempt to make light of the situation.

Reversing. You are blamed for the problem.

The Put-off. Your need to express your anger is met with "Sue me" or "I'll talk about it later." Of course, later never comes.

Retaliation. Your anger is responded to with a personal attack, such as "I'll get back at you even worse next time."

Why? Everything you say is responded to with a series of "why" questions, such as "Why do you feel that way?" "Why is that important?" "Why didn't you tell me before?"

Threats. You are threatened with statements like "So, I'll leave if you don't like it" or "If you keep nagging me, kiss our marriage good-bye."

Denial. You are told "That's not true; I didn't do that" or "That's your opinion."

Guilt. The person responds with tears and the message that you are being mean and cruel. "How could you say such things to me?"

Squabbling. The person wants to debate with you about the legitimacy of what you feel, or the magnitude of the problem: "Well, you shouldn't feel that way. I don't think it's fair for you to say that."

Here are some work-out techniques that are *proven* ways for overcoming the above blocking gambits and examples of when they can be used.

Play it again. Repeat your point calmly instead of getting sidetracked by irrelevant issues: "Yes, I know, but my point is . . ." "Yes, but I was saying . . ." Use with Humor and the Put-off.

Processing. Shift the focus of the discussion from the topic, and comment on what is going on between the two of you: "We're getting off the point now. It seems we're getting into old issues instead of the present one." Use with Threats, Why?, and Laughing it off.

Hedging. You appear to give ground without actually doing so. Agree with the person's argument but don't agree to change: "That's a good point. I probably could be more attentive. Perhaps I could be neater." Use with Reversing and Retaliation.

Defusing. Ignoring the *content* of a person's act and putting off further discussion until he has calmed down. "I can see that you're very upset and angry right now; let's discuss it later this evening." To make this effective, you must really discuss the issue later. Use with Retaliation.

Cutoff. Respond to the provocative statement with only a short word, and quickly get back to the point. This helps prevent escalation: Yes, no, maybe. Use with Threats.

Knowing how to overcome the gambits that people use will help you stick to the issues at hand without becoming unglued. You will then have a strong *De*-fense against defensiveness.

WORK-OUT NOTE

All the techniques are based on the same strategy: The best way to overcome defensiveness is not to be defensive too. When you communicate nondefensively, you are not experiencing anger arousal. This makes it easier for you to think of alternative ways to get your message across and cope with defensive and angry behavior. When you get defensive, you cannot do this as well, probably not at all.

When All Else Fails

One of the advantages of being human is that we need not always be victims of our environment or circumstances. We have the kind of intelligence that allows us to control our own responses. It is the behavior of others that we cannot control. Many times, for example, we direct our anger and overcome blocking gambits but to no avail. The other person still continues the provoking behavior. In fact, it would be naïve to think that directing our anger is a cure-all. The harsh reality is that the target of our anger, more often than not, will continue to provoke us. For the times when directing our anger is not enough, the best workout strategy is to change *our* behavior rather than trying to change someone else's. Here are two things you can do independent of the provocation that will help you work out your anger when all else fails. (Neither one is particularly easy to implement.)

Learning to live with it

Accepting the fact that the other person or situation is not going to change is difficult for most people because it involves learning to accept disappointments and giving up the hope that things will be different. However, being able to do this works out anger because it frees you from putting your energy into a situation that constantly frustrates and provokes you. You can then focus on learning to respond to the person or situation in a way that is less anger arousing. The best way to implement "learning to live with it" is to mentally change the expectations that you have about the person's changing the provoking behavior. For example, instead of getting angry over your spouse's constant promise to be honest with you, accept the fact that he or she is unable to be totally honest with you. Paradoxically, many people find that once they learn to live with it, other people do change their behavior—but don't count on it.

WORK-OUT NOTE

The reason why "learning to live with it" is thought to facilitate changing the other person depends on the psychological theory one uses. A well-accepted notion is that one person attempting to change the other typically leads to a power struggle, which causes resistance to change. Learning to live with it dissipates the power struggle, thus allowing people to change on their own.

Setting self-limits

Many people cannot learn to live with it. Their attitude is "Why should I have to put up with this?" or more simply, "I can't accept it." For these people, the best way to work out their anger is to decide how much or for how long they will allow themselves to tolerate a provoking behavior or situation. When that point is reached, they leave the situation. The key to setting self-limits, and being able to implement them, is preparing yourself for the worse so you can accept it if need be. Once you are willing to accept the worst (which is never as bad as you believe it to be), you have the psychological strength to follow through because you know you can handle it. When people fail to prepare for the worst, they end up staying in a provoking situation that they cannot live with, which makes them angrier and angrier and eventually leads to feelings of helplessness and depression.

Learning to live with it and setting self-limits are not easy to do but they are effective methods for working out anger.

As you learn to express your anger without blaming and shaming and to overcome the other B.S. that impedes anger resolution, you will find yourself becoming a lot happier. And that's no B.S.!

TAKE ACTION

1. Fill out the Anger Style Chart. Your responses will help you determine how you express your anger with the significant people in your life. To increase the chart's validity, think of the last two times you got angry at each person and how you expressed it. If you cannot remember past anger incidents, then observe how you express your anger the next time you get angry at each person.

Person	Escalate	Stuff	Direct
Spouse	_____	_____	_____
Children	_____	_____	_____
Parents	_____	_____	_____
Boss	_____	_____	_____
Co-worker	_____	_____	_____
Friends (who)	_____	_____	_____

What styles do you tend to use the most?

Think about why you escalate in some situations and stuff in others.

Think of some specific things you can do to make your anger style more productive.

2. Think about the following people toward whom you might express anger and the blocking gambits they use. Then write down how you will overcome them the next time they use them.

Person	Gambits	How you will overcome them
Spouse	_____	_____
Children	_____	_____
Mother	_____	_____
Father	_____	_____
Boss	_____	_____
Friends (who)	_____	_____

3. Think of a constant provoking behavior or situation and then think of a change that *you* can make when all else fails.

THE BIGGEST MISTAKE PEOPLE MAKE
IN THIS WORK-OUT IS

to forget they still have options when directing their anger is ineffective. They then end up escalating or stuffing.

W O R K - O U T   N O T E S

_____

_____

_____

_____

_____

_____

_____

_____

_____

_____

_____

ANGER WORK-OUT #9

Being a Real Cool Hand

Recommended for:
1. *People who have coronary problems*
2. *People who frequently get angry*
3. *People who are frequently tense and irritable*
4. *People who experience a lot of aggravation*
5. *People who are impatient*
6. *People who have stressful jobs*
7. *People who want to live longer and healthier*
8. *People who want to be peak performers*

PURPOSE

At some time in your life, especially when you have been angry, someone has told you to "relax," or "calm down." This was excellent advice. When you can relax, your blood pressure, pulse rate, perspiration and respiration rates decrease, reactions that are antagonistic to intense anger arousal.

Few of us, however, have been taught the "whats" and "hows" that will enable us to consciously relax when necessary. This is true even though being able to relax definitely helps us live longer and improve the quality of our lives.

Anger Work-out #9 teaches you how to consciously relax, how to develop your *relaxation response*. Then you can be cool, calm, and collected, even in the heat of anger.

INFORMATION

Your Relaxation Response—What It Does

Your relaxation response (RR) is a protective mechanism to counter the harmful physical and mental effects of anger. Specifically, learning to use your RR helps you do the following:

Avoid intense anger arousal

When you have developed your RR, you will be able to use it to short-circuit anger arousal *before* it becomes too intense. Using your RR like this helps you control your anger.

Appraise the situation accurately

By keeping your anger from becoming intense, your RR enables you to appraise the situation accurately, something you *cannot* do during intense anger arousal. When you can be angry and *still* appraise the situation accurately, you can convert the anger arousal you experience into the energy you need to confront the provocation productively. Being able to use your RR so that you can think clearly *when* you are angry is the essential difference between being able to use your anger productively and letting your anger paralyze you.

Develop a new anger tape

Almost all of us experience anger's negative aftermath—guilt, shame, embarrassment, depression, anxiety, and other distressful reactions that cause us to *get* angrier because we *got* angry. Most of these reactions stem from the actual consequences of how we express anger and the fact that we have also been programmed to think of anger as a negative response. "Getting angry is wrong. Don't do it" is the tape that our cerebral computer plays. As you practice and develop your relaxation response, you will have the opportunity to create a new "anger tape" by continually programming into your subconscious, while you are physically relaxed, the mental message that it is often acceptable to be angry and that anger can be used for productive gains. Because your RR physically and mentally relaxes you, your subconscious becomes more receptive to new data. This new subconscious tape will be reinforced every time you work out. This is one of the principles used in hypnosis.

WORK-OUT NOTE

> The work-out process uses the term *subconscious* to refer to that part of your thinking system that controls your beliefs—your data bank. Once data has been programmed into your data bank, it is rarely, if ever, challenged as to its validity. This makes it almost impossible for people to feel good about their thoughts, feelings, and behavior when they contradict how they have been programmed. Creating a new anger tape and entering it into your data bank will free you from the myth that it's wrong to get angry.

Improve and optimize your life

Your RR helps you work out your anger. But there are also other benefits to reap. For example, there are hundreds of studies that indicate that using your RR will benefit your total health. Decreasing your chances of having a heart attack, developing hypertension, or becoming obese or alcoholic, and improving your productivity in work are just a few of the numerous benefits associated with using your RR.

Your Relaxation Response—How It Works

Your RR works on a physical level and on a psychological level.

The physical level

Humans react in a predictable way to acute and chronic stressful situations that trigger the inborn part of our physiological makeup called the fight-or-flight response. When we encounter situations that challenge our survival, the fight-flight response increases our blood pressure, heart rate, rate of respiration, blood flow to the muscles, and metabolism, all of which prepares us for either direct conflict or escape. However, the fight-flight response is frequently not used as intended—that is, in preparation for running or for fighting with an enemy, a survival mechanism. It is frequently brought on by situations that require us to make behavioral adjustments—a new job, loss of a job, death of a loved one, divorce, marriage, change of financial status. When the fight-flight response is invoked inappropriately—which is most of the time—and when it is used repeatedly, it can lead to disturbed health.

Anger as an emotion is a derivative of the fight-flight response. This is why people who experience frequent and intense outbursts of the emotion are prone to adverse physical conditions—they are using the fight-flight response inappropriately. By developing your RR, you can counteract the increased sympathetic-nervous-system activity that accompanies the arousal of the fight-flight response, i.e., anger arousal. You can then restore your body to its normal balance.

WORK-OUT NOTE

Dr. Walter Rudolph Hess, a Swiss physiologist and Nobel Prize winner, provided the first *empirical* evidence of a relaxation response when he found that sending an electrical current to one part of a cat's hypothalamus stimulated an increase in heart rate and pupillary dilation, but stimulation to another part produced just the opposite. It is now known that relaxation can be intentionally induced by activities that decrease sympathetic-nervous-system activity by programming the hypothalamus to trigger lower blood pressure and a reduced heart rate. A relaxation response decreases oxygen consumption and carbon-dioxide elimination. The heart and breathing rates simultaneously slow. Blood flow to the muscles is stabilized. The state is one of a quiet, restful relaxation.

The psychological level

You can develop your RR by associating specific thoughts and images with a specific physiological state (relaxation). There is nothing magical about developing your RR. The conditioning process it uses is a law of science, and simply requires practice. In an anger-arousing situation, thinking of your "relaxation image" or verbalizing your "relaxing self-statements" will evoke your RR, which will then counteract your anger arousal and keep you in charge.

WORK-OUT NOTE

Although people have been using such techniques for thousands of years, Dr. Herbert Benson is generally credited with coining the phrase "relaxation response." Benson is best known for pinpointing the elements that appear crucial to developing a relaxation response independent of the relaxation exercise used. However, Benson's work implies that one should practice relaxation daily in order to relieve the daily stresses (appropriate and inappropriate) that we all encounter. Although the work-out process also emphasizes using a relaxation response on a daily basis, the major emphasis is on using the relaxation response as an intervention—an optional way of responding—in anger-arousing situations. Hence, daily usage is recommended so that one can "automatically" use the relaxation response as needed. In this sense, the work-out process is really advocating the development of a *conditioned* relaxation response (CRR) rather than simply relaxation for the sake of relaxation.

Your Relaxation Response—The Essentials

There are numerous techniques that you can use to develop your RR, such as Transcendental Meditation, Zen, yoga, progressive relaxation, self-hypnosis, autogenic training, and biofeedback. There are however, four essential components that, irrespective of method, are thought to be necessary to develop your RR.

A *quiet environment*. When developing your RR, choose a quiet, calm environment without distractions. This will make it easier to avoid interfering stimuli when you are focusing on your RR images and/or statements.

A *mental device*. Having a mental device—a sound, word, image, statement, fixed gaze—helps you shift your mind from being externally oriented to being internally oriented. This is important because it enables you to "feel" what is going on in your body. Having a constant word or image also helps you overcome a major problem in developing your RR—mind wandering. Saying the word "breaks" your distracting thoughts. It is very important to remember to use the *same* image, word, sound—or other mental device—each time you practice your RR. This consistency will *strengthen* the association between your thoughts and the desired level of physiological arousal. When you are inconsistent, your mental device does not achieve the power it needs to evoke the relaxed feeling. Thus, using the same mental device helps you develop the RR on a psychological level.

A passive attitude. Passivity is probably the most important component in developing your RR. Distracting thoughts will occur. Do not worry when this happens, just return to your mental device. If you worry about how well you are doing, you may prevent the RR from happening. Adapt a "let it happen" attitude. Distracting thoughts *do not mean* that you are doing something incorrectly. They are to be expected.

A comfortable position. When you practice your RR, it is important to be in a comfortable position so that there is no undue muscular tension. If a position gets uncomfortable, it is a signal that tension is increasing. Switch to a position that makes you feel more comfortable.

These are the essentials that are required to develop your RR. As mentioned earlier, there are numerous techniques available. The work-out process uses the following relaxation exercise because it is brief and it has all the essentials covered. Read it a few times so you can do it on your own. It takes approximately fifteen minutes to do it. You will first exaggerate muscle tensions before relaxing them. Do the following steps one at a time.

1. Clench your fist . . . tighter, tighter . . . relax.
2. Suck in your stomach; try to make it touch your back. Hold it. Relax.
3. Clench your teeth, lock your jaws . . . firmer . . . firmer . . . relax.
4. Close your eyelids tightly. Force them together more and more. Release.
5. Push your head and neck into your shoulders. Farther down. Release
6. Inhale. Hold it as long as you can. Release.
7. Stretch out your arms and legs . . . stiffer . . . stiffer . . . release.
8. Now do all seven steps together. Release and let a warm, soft wave flow over your body, relaxing each part in turn as it slowly moves from your head down around over and into every muscle. Especially let it loosen the tension around your eyes, forehead, mouth, neck, and back. Tension out, relaxation in. Let the wave of gentle relaxation dissolve all muscle tension.

Open your eyes. Hold your thumbnail a few inches from your eyes and focus all attention on it. Your hand will come down slowly. As it does, allow your eyelids to get heavy, your breathing to become fuller, and your whole body to enter a deep state of relaxation. Eyes closed, hands down at your sides or on your lap. Breathe in and out deeply, with each breath counting to yourself. One . . . deeper, two . . . deeper, three . . . deeper, and up to ten (very deeply relaxed). Now imagine yourself in the most relaxing situation possible. See it, feel it, hear it, smell it, touch it. Float on a raft on a warm summer day, or in a hot bath. Go for a walk in the forest after a refreshing morning rain. Whatever your relaxation image is, go to it. Now your body and mind are prepared for the message of the day. "When I am becoming angry, it pays to relax myself so I can use my anger to my best advantage. Anger can help me grow. It can help me express my feelings and make my relationships better. It can prevent and resolve conflicts instead of making them worse. It can be a source of energy so that I can use it to help me accomplish the task at hand. When someone is angry at me, it means that they need to talk with me, not that they don't love me or that they want to hurt me. Their anger is a cue that it is time for me to help them." Enjoy the good mental state and the relaxed physical state. Before counting yourself out of the relaxation state (saying ten, nine, eight, seven . . .) be aware of how good it now feels to be you and how you are gaining control of your thoughts, feelings, and actions. Tell yourself that this awareness and the positive feelings will persist through the next time you are angry. You might want to throw in a key word to help you return to this relaxed state when you are getting angry. Now bring yourself out.

People differ in how long it takes them to develop their RR but if you practice ten to fifteen minutes a day, you can feel results within two weeks.

Your Relaxation Response—When To Use It

Here are some times when you can use your RR:

Every day. Using and practicing your RR every day will make your daily life less stressful. This in itself will cause you to cut down on needless and unjust anger. You will also be able to perform your daily activities much better, and your health, in all probability, will improve. Practicing your RR every day also ensures that you will be able to use it when you need it.

When you feel tense or irritable. At the first signs of feeling tense and irritable, use your RR. This will prevent full-blown anger from developing.

When someone expresses anger to you. Using your RR here will prevent you from escalating the situation, and allow you to listen to the person without being defensive. As he sees you "relaxed" and paying attention, he is more likely to calm down too.

When you know you will encounter a provocation. If you know you are going to confront an anger-arousing situation, make sure you use your RR. It will help you stay in control and appraise the situation accurately. Most people who use their RR *before* they encounter the provocation find that the provoking situation isn't that provoking after all.

As you begin to use your RR more and more, you will immunize yourself against intense anger arousal. You will also get rid of one of your provocations: people telling you to relax or calm down!

TAKE ACTION

1. Write down a time that you will take a relaxation break on a daily basis.
    _____

2. For the next two weeks, practice the relaxation exercise every day. Be sure you are in a comfortable position and in a quiet place where you will not be disturbed.

3. Write down the key word you told yourself or the image you held while you were relaxed. These are your relaxation statements and image. Memorize them and use them in anger and stress situations.

    _____

    _____

4. List three situations in which your relaxation response will help you. Be sure to use your relaxation response when you are in these situations.

    _____

    _____

    _____

5. Make a little sign with your relaxation word. Keep it in your daily environments— on your office desk, on your night table, in your car, and any other place you spend a lot of time.

THE BIGGEST MISTAKE PEOPLE MAKE
IN THIS WORK-OUT IS

not practicing their RR for a sufficient period of time. After trying it for three days, they say, "It doesn't work." This is correct. You need approximately two weeks of practice for the conditioning process to work. Remember, conditioning yourself is part of any good work-out.

WORK-OUT NOTES

_____

_____

_____

_____

_____

_____

_____

_____

_____

_____

ANGER WORK-OUT #10

Time Bomb

Recommended for:
1. *People who get angry and don't know why*
2. *People who get ticked off easily*
3. *People who want to avoid unnecessary anger*
4. *People who are chronically angry*
5. *People who want to be able to manage the worst and do their best*

PURPOSE

Knowing your provocations benefits you because:

- You can develop a work-out strategy in *advance* for coping with the provocation the next time you confront it. This helps abort your anger.
- You can learn how to avoid certain provocations altogether, or at least have minimum exposure to them and thereby prevent anger.
- When you can identify your provocations, you can begin to arrange them in order of the severity of your response. You are then able to practice coping skills and strategies with your milder provocations, and build up your confidence and skill for coping with your major provocations when you actually encounter them.

In short, Anger Work-out #10 helps you identify your provocations so you know what ticks you off. Then you can watch for your anger and defuse your bomb before it explodes.

WORK-OUT NOTE

When you know what provokes you, you can reflect on each provocation and (re)appraise it in the *absence* of anger arousal and anger actions. This makes you *less* susceptible to the cognitive distortions that you make when you do experience anger arousal and anger actions. When your thinking is free of cognitive distortions, and you are not experiencing anger arousal or anger actions, it becomes much easier to break your anger feedback loops. You are then able to generate a new and productive response for your next confrontation.

INFORMATION

Identifying Your Provocations

Our individual provocations may be classified into the following provocation categories:

Frustrations. A frustration occurs when you try to do something and are prevented, blocked, or disappointed. The psychology adage "Frustration leads to aggression" is too frequently true.

Irritations and Annoyances. These are incidents that get on your nerves, such as noise or frequent interruptions.

Abuse. We get angry when someone abuses us, either verbally or physically. Verbal abuse consists of name-calling, cursing, and other unkind remarks that are directed to us. Sometimes the abusive remark is very obvious and direct, and other times it is more a subtle attack. Physical abuse, like pushing, grabbing, punching, or kicking occurs less frequently than verbal abuse.

Injustice or unfairness. These are situations where you have not been treated fairly or received what you deserved, for example, when someone accuses you without hearing your side of the story.

The work-out process instructs you to classify your individual provocations into one of the four categories because *the act of classifying assists you in examining reactions.* For example, if you got angry because you didn't get a promotion, is that a frustration, an injustice, or abuse? The only way you can decide is to appraise the event and the self-statements that you make. Furthermore, when you classify your provocations, you will begin to recognize many of your cognitive distortions (a skill that will be sharpened in Anger Work-out #6) that fueled the anger experience. These hot cognitions can then be cooled down the next time you encounter the provocations. Finally, knowing what category your individual provocations fall into will help you decide what work-out strategy to use. For example, dealing with anger created by frustration is quite different from dealing with anger created by abuse.

As you think about your provocations, you will realize that what provokes you does not necessarily provoke someone else. This is because different people can appraise the same event differently. Research has shown, however, that in almost all marriages (and live-in relationships) there are common provocations. In order of anger-provoking frequency, these provocations are:

- Money
- Indifference to mate's feelings
- Sex/adultery
- Irresponsibility
- Drinking

These concerns are so provoking that in about half of all families, discussion of them reaches the hitting or shoving stage at least once. In one out of ten families, discussion of these subjects leads one mate to hit another with an object, and about one in twenty-six women suffers regular physical abuse. Therefore, it becomes essential that you start to think about what you will do the next time these common provocations—as well as your unique ones—arise.

WORK-OUT NOTE

You will find that many times your "solutions" for working out a provocation are ineffective. The trick is to continue trying alternative ways of responding until you get the results you need—remember the concept of operant learning. However, make sure you give each solution a fair chance. As you move through the work-out process, you will get better at developing effective strategies for dealing with your provocations.

Copycating

Copycating offers an effective technique to practice confronting your provocations without losing control so that you will be more confident when you confront them in real life.

One of the most effective ways to learn a new behavior is to observe and imitate someone else doing it successfully. A shy individual can watch someone initiate a conversation and then imitate the "model." Copycating, then, relies upon this most basic type of learning—not by watching real-life models, but by creating and patterning ourselves after the perfect and rich images we envision. By identifying, refining, and practicing in our minds the necessary steps for successfully confronting a provocation, it becomes easier to confront the provocation in real life. In short, we "copy" the behavior that we have already carried out in our minds.

A good way to use copycating is to arrange your provocations in order of the severity of your response. In a comfortable setting, relax yourself and then visualize yourself successfully confronting each provocation. To be a real copycat, do the following:

- Start with the least severe provocation. Make sure you have a vivid picture of where you are and who is with you. Use your senses of sound and smell to make it sharper.

- Hold on to the provoking image for thirty to forty seconds and be aware of how your body reacts: changes in your heart rate and breathing, and particularly the beginning of any muscle tension. Use these responses as cues to take a deep breath and to breathe more slowly. The changes your body makes are like a warning of what later will be real anger. If you appraise the feelings of arousal in your body as anger, you will experience anger. But if you can use the same arousal as a *cue* to relax, you can begin immediately to start managing your anger productively. Most people who work out are able to relax away the anger even as they imagine a particularly provoking situation.

- Keep your provocation scene very visual, and at the same time breathe slowly and deeply to help you relax. Occasionally, imagine yourself losing control and starting to respond angrily. Use the loss of control as a cue to increase your coping efforts. Imagine having the impulse to really blow up, then inhibiting the impulse and deciding not to attack. Then return to visualizing success.

- Stick with the provoking scene until you can think of it *without* experiencing any discomfort. If you do experience your habitual response, continue to visualize yourself coping effectively.

- When you have visualized a particular provocation scene three times without experiencing *any* anger arousal, go on to the next item and repeat the procedure. As you practice, you will gain important knowledge of how and where your anger builds up in your body. You will find that using the early signs of tension as a cue to relax is extremely valuable in all parts of your life.

WORK-OUT NOTE

Copycating is based on the well-validated assumption that imagery can evoke the same response an individual makes in reality. Consider the research by physiologist Edmund Jacobson, who has shown that when an individual vividly imagines running, there are small but measurable contractions in his muscles, comparable to the changes that occur during actual running. Similarly, by holding a rich, provoking image in your mind you can raise your blood pressure, accelerate your pulse and perspiration rate, and elicit dryness of the mouth. Copycating has been found to improve scores of behaviors for all types of people, including children. In the business and sports worlds, its use is now motivating careers and promoting success. It is well known that all the Olympic champions visualized winning gold medals, and there are numerous stories of how successful businessmen visualized their success. Conrad Hilton said that he visualized himself running a hotel many years before he purchased his first one.

Avoiding the Worst

Identifying your provocations enables you to use another technique—avoidant strategies. This is a creative way for getting the results you need while bypassing the provocation. Do not confuse an avoidant strategy with "running away" from a problem. Shortening extended visits with parents to preserve their pleasure and avoid the predictable hassles that come with spending too much time together, and shopping at a different time to avoid the frustration and anger of standing in line are good examples of avoidant strategies. The way to develop an avoidant strategy is simple. Just write down a provocation, and next to it list different ways you can still get what you need without having to confront the provocation, or by escaping the situation before it becomes provoking. This requires some thinking time but it's worth it to avoid the worst.

As you continue doing Anger Work-out #10, not only will you learn how to deal effectively with your "time bombs" before they set you off but you will also develop skills you can apply "spontaneously" to new anger-arousing situations. This alone will cut down on the number of times you come home in a lousy mood. You are on your way to becoming an anger athlete!

TAKE ACTION

1. Give yourself a couple of days to think about your five most common and intense provocations. List them according to how severely you respond to them and categorize them into a provocation category. Note any cognitive distortions you are making. Then write down for each one something you can do that will help you manage your anger the next time you are confronted.

Provocation (most intense)	Provocation Category	Coping Strategy
1. _____	_____	_____
2. _____	_____	_____
3. _____	_____	_____
4. _____	_____	_____
5. _____	_____	_____

2. Use copycating with your provocation list.

3. Develop an avoidant strategy for as many of your provocations as you can.

Get started here:

Provocation: _____

Avoidant Strategy: _____

Provocation: _____

Avoidant Strategy: _____

THE BIGGEST MISTAKE PEOPLE MAKE
IN THIS WORK-OUT IS

to deny their provocations are really provoking because, in retrospect, they do not seem to make them angry. These people then reason that working out is not necessary. They fail to realize that the purpose of Anger Work-out #10 is to help you work out anger by preparing for it when you are not angry. Without preparation, your anger returns when the provocation returns.

W O R K - O U T   N O T E S

_____

_____

_____

_____

_____

_____

_____

_____

_____

_____

ANGER WORK-OUT #11

You Are What You Expect

PURPOSE

Expectations are the mental "bets" we make with ourselves about the outcome of future events, our behavior, and the behavior of others. They often reflect our goals and standards.

Our expectations are a powerful force in determining our behavior and how we respond to others. Anger, acute or chronic anger, is frequently related to the expectations that we have for ourselves and others, and for the situations we encounter.

Anger Work-out #11 will help clarify the role expectations play in your anger experiences, and will help make your expectations work for you.

WORK-OUT NOTE

You have no doubt heard the phrase "self-fulfilling prophecy"—if you believe something about yourself (or others), you tend to make it happen by acting in accordance with your belief. The self-fulfilling prophecy has been validated by thousands of empirical studies. The finding to be used here is that being aware of your expectations gives you greater control of your behavior.

INFORMATION

When to "Expect" Anger

Here are some ways in which expectations about ourselves and others make us more prone to experiencing anger:

- High expectations of ourselves that are not met cause us to get angry. Most people believe it is important to have high expectations. But when the results we anticipate do not ensue, we become frustrated and irritable. To make matters worse, the results we get are often appraised in a negative light, and we end up not giving ourselves the positive strokes we really deserve. Logic to the contrary, the message we give ourselves is that we are a *total* failure because we didn't achieve our goal. The result is destructive anger that lowers our self-esteem.
- Our high expectations of others cause us to get angry and lead to interpersonal conflict. Think of times you expected your lover to do something and he didn't do it—whether it was having dinner ready, acting lovingly, or asking you about your day. Chances are his failing to meet your expectation provoked anger.
- High expectations that someone will continue to act in a way we have found objectionable in the past is likely to make our anger more intense and more frequent. This may lead to anticipatory anger—becoming angry *before* the other person does or says anything. Thinking that your lover is going to continue his "inconsiderate behavior" will only increase your anger-provoking self-statements—"He'll never change." "He will always treat me like this"—and have the effect of making you experience needless anger and be more susceptible to expressing unjust anger. Expecting someone to do something you don't like also makes you

hypersensitive to signs that he is going to behave in this way. These signs provoke anger even before the person actually acts provokingly. If you are angry that your mate is overweight and believe she will not adhere to her new diet (as usual), you will probably begin to get angry if you see her go into the kitchen. You expect her to eat, but in reality, she may be cleaning up or looking for something other than food. In such situations premature anger undermines the person's honest attempt to change her behavior. It makes the other person feel as though you lack confidence in her and threatens a trusting relationship. Furthermore, your anger often triggers the other person's anger, which may be all she needs to actually do what you object to. In this case, eating more.

• Low expectations that you can handle a particular situation will increase your chances of becoming angry. Telling yourself that you "can't do it" brings to life the self-fulfilling prophecy. Whether it's a meeting with your boss or ex-wife, or taking an examination, lack of confidence in your ability to cope will lower your frustration level and increase your chances of reacting with anger. Low expectations make you give up easily and become frustrated quickly. Lacking the patience to try alternative responses, or lacking the confidence that you will succeed, you find yourself at your wits' end. Anger comes out of desperation.

You can see how expectations may create problems for you. High or low, they can provoke your anger. Since it's impossible to avoid expectations, your best bet is to be realistic in your expectations.

WORK-OUT NOTE

As you learn to make your expectations work for you, they will assist you in combating at least two of the distorted thinking styles—Shoulding and Magnification. Our high expectations are usually manifested as "You should have," or "I should have." Low self-expectations tend to exaggerate your inability to handle a situation or accomplish a specific task or goal—"I'll never be able to do it," "I can't handle this." This is a good example of how the work-outs build on each other.

Identifying Expectations

The first step in making your expectations realistic and getting them to work for you is to identify them. When you identify your expectations, you give yourself the opportunity to appraise them accurately. Once you have identified your expectations, the following strategies will help you decide if they are realistic:

- Use past similar experiences as your base line. If you expect your business or income to double over the next year, but past experience shows the best you've ever done is a 15 percent increase, you are probably setting yourself up for disappointment (realistically, a 25 percent increase would be terrific and a 20 percent increase would still be great progress). If you are starting a new diet and expect to lose three pounds a week, and past experience shows the best you've ever done before is a weekly loss of a pound and a half, your expectations are too high (a two-pound weekly loss would be great). If you expect your lover to have dinner ready when you come home, and past experience shows that this happens only on weekends, chances are you'll get angry as soon as you see the table. By using past experiences as your data base, you have a valid method for forming realistic expectations.

- Ask others what they think. Sometimes it's difficult to be honest with yourself. Sharing expectations that you have of yourself with other people gives you feedback as to whether or not you are being too hard (or easy) on yourself. They can help you evaluate expectations in terms of realism.

- Assign percentages to your expected outcomes. Quantifying the chances for your "expected" outcomes (60 percent chance, 50 percent chance, 20 percent chance) helps you think clearly as to whether you really believe the expectation is going to be met. Once you assign a percentage to your expectation, you can modify it as the situation evolves, and in the process develop a realistic outlook. This illustrates an important point: Expectations will serve you best when they are elastic rather than static.

W O R K - O U T   N O T E

Making expectations realistic does not mean you should not set them high. The perennial track star, a best-selling author, and a movie star all have exceedingly high expectations for themselves. Yet their past behavior dictates that they are realistic. But for the average high-school star, the first-time author, and the novice actor, the same expectations would be unrealistic, to say the least.

Communicating Expectations

Letting other people know what you expect of them is a characteristic of the most productive relationships and effective organizations. Letting people know what is expected of them gives them the opportunity to *validate* whether or not your expectation is realistic—if they feel they can meet it. If they think they can't, they are able to explain their viewpoint, and together you can reach a "realistic expectation." This prevents you from having unrealistically high expectations of others, and saves you from needless and unjust anger. Letting people know what you expect of them also provides them with important information about you—such as what you think is important, and what your needs are.

Everyone has expectations. And when you can identify, clarify, and communicate yours, you can begin to "expect" that they will work for you!

TAKE ACTION

1. Think of a recent incident in which you got angry at yourself and note the expectations you had for yourself. Were they realistic? How do you know?

2. List two expectations you have for yourself. Are they realistic? How do you know?

   _____

   _____

3. List two expectations that you have for your lover. Are they realistic? How do you know? Show them to your lover to see what he or she thinks.

   _____

   _____

4. Ask your lover what he or she expects from you and see if these are realistic expectations.

THE BIGGEST MISTAKE PEOPLE MAKE
IN THIS WORK-OUT IS

that they "expect" other people to know what they expect of them. This mistake is double trouble. For one thing, having this expectation reflects an imperative thinking style—You should know what I expect. For another, it asks other people to practice mind reading, and when they are "wrong," you get angry at them. You can avoid this mistake by communicating your expectations.

WORK-OUT NOTES

_____

_____

_____

_____

_____

_____

_____

_____

_____

_____

ANGER WORK-OUT #12

Your "A" Team

PURPOSE

Getting a friend to go to the gym or start an exercise class with you is a smart move. It makes working out easier and more fun, and most important, you and your friend can support one another's efforts to get in shape. Mutual support is a valuable source of energy for keeping you committed to working out.

Almost anything is easier when you feel emotionally supported, and working out anger is no exception. In fact, nothing is lonelier, harder, or more stressful than having to deal with emotional pain without some type of help. Having a reliable support team to aid and abet your efforts, especially for those times when you are really hurting, will help renew and revitalize your desire to get your "self" in shape.

Anger Work-out #12 will help you develop a support team that you can use daily. It will also help you improve your interpersonal relationships.

INFORMATION

Building Your Team

Select your team members on the basis of two qualities: trust and availability.

Trust is important because it promotes comfort in expressing your thoughts and feelings. When trust is low, it becomes difficult to get support because you do not let the other people know what it is that is really bothering you. Thus they cannot respond to the real issue, let alone give you the support you need. You will find that you trust different people with different parts of your life. For example, with one friend, you may feel comfortable discussing your intimate relationships but not your financial affairs. With another friend, it may be just the opposite. Areas of your life where you will probably need support include work, marriage or intimate relationships, finances, social life, parental relationships, and sibling relationships. Knowing in advance whom you can talk to about what will allow you to get in touch instantly when you need help and prevent you from feeling "There's nobody I can talk to."

Availability is important because it increases your speed for getting support. As you build your team, you may find that you are excluding people who are highly trustworthy. Parents who live in another state, or a friend you don't see often, may be trustworthy, but if they are not very available to you, they will not be much use to you on a weekly basis. For this reason, you are probably better off using people you associate with rather than family or close friends who live a thousand miles away. It is also a good idea to build a team that has at least four people so that there will always be someone who can give you support.

You can improve your team by increasing the trust factor, increasing the availability level, and broadening the number of areas you can talk about with each team member. The secret for doing this is using your team.

Using Your Team

Your team can be of no help to you unless you use them. Start by letting them know:

- You are actively trying to learn how to use your anger to work for you.

- In order to do this, you have to do "work-outs" on a daily basis.
- You would appreciate their support in your efforts to do the work-outs.
- Periodically asking you about your anger work-out program would be beneficial.
- There will be times when you discuss "anger incidents" with them and they can help you by encouraging you to work them out.
- You would appreciate knowing how they feel about supporting you. Because these are people you already trust and share some intimacy with, they will most likely be glad to help you.
- You might want to get them a copy of the *Anger Work-out Book* to show them what you are doing and to get them to work out with you!

Remember, it's important not to let yourself come to rely on just one person—the strategy here is to build options so that you can get good support from a variety of people.

Here are some specific ways to use your "team."

Putting it in perspective

When we get angry, we almost always see things "out of perspective." Your team can help you put things "in perspective" and make it easier for you to work out.

- Tell them what happened.
- Tell them what you think.
- Ask them what they think.
- Reappraise the situation.

Bouncing board

Instead of using your team as a sounding board to ventilate your anger (which will sometimes increase it), use your team for "bouncing around your feelings."

- Use statements beginning with "I feel . . ."
- Ask them how they would feel in a similar situation. This helps you realize you are not alone in your feelings.
- Think about your feelings after you have "bounced them around."

Problem solving

Instead of complaining to your team about the hopelessness of a situation, use them to help you solve problems.

- Tell them the problem and how you've tried to solve it.
- Ask them for solutions.
- Reappraise the problem and solution.

Using your team is the best way to improve it. Every time you call on the members, you are strengthening your trust in them and increasing your level of intimacy. Because you trust them, you are also going to feel that you can be honest in talking about your anger incidents and feelings with them. This sense of honesty will further increase your trust and deepen your level of intimacy.

Supporting Your Team

The best way to *get* support is to *give* it by demonstrating to each team member that support is mutual. In fact, the only way your team can survive is for you to support each of them when necessary. Otherwise, they will start to feel that you are too selfish and you may end up being a BIG pain in the butt. Mutual support bonds your relationship. Here are some ways to build support:

- Ask each member what's going on in his life. This shows that you care, and their self-disclosing answers promote intimacy.
- Frequently ask nonthreatening questions about some aspect of their lives that you want to support them in—work relationships, parents, etc. This creates an "area" that they will feel they can talk about with you.
- Acknowledge the continuity of their lives by following through on past conversations—"How did that job interview go?" "What did Irv say about your mother?" This shows that you listened.
- Demonstrate to your team members that you think about them—sending birthday cards, cards from trips, calls just to say hello.
- Demonstrate to your team how you feel about them by talking about the positive feelings you have for them. This nourishes your relationship.
- Periodically ask if they need you to do anything—help with

a party, pick something up at a special store, help them move, etc.
- Start out your next conversation with each team member with "How are you feeling?"

Building mutually supportive relationships with each of your team members will develop tremendous emotional strength for everybody. You and your team will want to support each other because it feels so good. You will be having super relationships with all of them. When this happens, you'll have your "A" team.

If you have no team

If you do not have the resources to build a team, but want one, you can build one from scratch. The strategy is simple but does require a lot of energy from you. Pick people whom you would like to know better. Then cultivate the relationships, focusing on honesty, intimacy, and trust. If this is difficult for you to do, start out by *acting* as though you trust the person. Trust someone with small things first and let it build. Mutual support will evolve!

TAKE ACTION

1. List all the people you can trust (but no more than ten) with one being most trust-worthy. Next to each person, rate the availability level (high, frequent, low) and the areas of your life that you feel comfortable in sharing with him or her. After you have done this, go down the availability column until you have counted four people who are either highly available or frequently available to you. Transfer these four names to the following Team Sheet and you will have your "A" Team.

	Trust	Availability	Topics
1.	_____	_____	_____
2.	_____	_____	_____
3.	_____	_____	_____
4.	_____	_____	_____
5.	_____	_____	_____
6.	_____	_____	_____
7.	_____	_____	_____
8.	_____	_____	_____
9.	_____	_____	_____
10.	_____	_____	_____

T E A M   S H E E T

Team Member	Topics	Phone#
I.		
II.		
III.		
IV.		

2. List one new way you can use your team.

_____

3. List one new way you can support your team.

_____

4. Go to an educational or social event to scout a new team member.

_____

THE BIGGEST MISTAKE PEOPLE MAKE
IN THIS WORK-OUT IS

to fail to support their team.

W O R K - O U T   N O T E S

_____

_____

_____

_____

_____

_____

_____

_____

_____

_____

_____

ANGER WORK-OUT #13

Puzzled? Finding the Missing Peace

> Recommended for:
> 1. People who have a lot of problems
> 2. People who can't solve their problems
> 3. People who are depressed
> 4. People who feel helpless and frustrated
> 5. People who want to be more creative

PURPOSE

Because of the complex and ever-changing nature of our society, people in the modern world find themselves continuously confronted by situational problems. Whether it's a problem as minor as trying to decide what tie or dress to wear each morning or a more significant issue, such as dealing with an unreasonable employee or a nagging spouse, or meeting mortgage payments, our daily lives are replete with problems that we must solve in order to maintain an adequate level of effective functioning. Depending upon the complexity of the situation, and the potential negative consequences of handling it poorly, these problems may be trivial or crucial.

Important problems that elude solutions become sources of chronic anger. If our usual coping strategies do not work, a growing sense of helplessness makes the search for novel solutions more difficult. The possibility of relief seems to recede; the problems become a puzzle that seems insoluble, causing us to experience frustration and chronic anger. All too often, our anger evolves into depression that cripples our ability to respond productively, leaving us to lead lives of quiet desperation.

Anger Work-out #13 will give you a problem-solving technique that will help you generate novel solutions to *ny* kind of problem. Even better, you can use it immediately.

Anger Work-out #13 is one of the most rigorous work-outs, but the peace it brings is well worth the effort.

INFORMATION

Understanding Problems

Life may be thought of as an endless series of situations that require some kind of response. Looking at it from this point of view, no situation is inherently a problem. It is the ineffectiveness of *your response* that makes it so. For example, the fact that you have misplaced an important paper and can't find it is not in itself a problem. It becomes a problem only if you neglect to look under the stack of papers on your desk where it is most likely to be found. If you look in your drawers and briefcase, on your car dashboard, you are *beginning* to create a problem—your response is not effective in finding the misplaced paper, and therefore the situation becomes a problem for you.

Sometimes you turn a situation into a problem by using a response that seems effective at the time, but proves to be disastrous in the long run. If you watch TV every night and your lover complains about it, you don't necessarily have a problem. You have a problem only if your response is ultimately ineffective. Your solution might be to discourage further comments by exploding whenever your lover interrupts. Such a plan would give you good results almost immediately. But over time, your lover might leave you or have an affair. Your solution had short term success but was ineffective in the long run. Evaluating the consequences of such false short-term solutions, and creating alternative responses that pay off in the long run, is part of finding the missing peace. This work-out teaches you to define problems not in terms of impossible situations but in terms of ineffective solutions. A good point to remember is that the problem is not the problem—the solution is the problem. As this statement begins to make sense to you, you will capture the essence of problem solving.

Becoming a Problem Solver

Learning to problem-solve is made easier when you adapt the Problem Solver's Outlook. This is based on the principle that an individual's general orientation or "set" in approaching a situation can greatly influence the way in which he will respond to that situation. The problem-solver's outlook *encourages* independent problem-solving behavior by having you do the following:

Accept the fact that problems constitute a normal part of life, and that it is possible to cope with most of these situations. This may be obvious, but people are inclined to think that it isn't OK to have problems. We see problems as something to hide as though to acknowledge them is to admit to personal failures. And how many times have you heard or thought "I don't want to burden you with my problems." This is the attitude of the poor problem solver.

Recognize problems when they occur. Even if you accept the complexities of the surrounding environment and are optimistic about your ability to handle various situations effectively, it may not always be easy to identify problems when they occur. Typically, we do not recognize that we have a problem until we find ourselves failing where we must succeed—where we cannot withdraw from the situation, or lower our standards, or ask for help, or throw a tantrum. This is when the poor problem solver knows he is in trouble. In contrast, the able problem solver recognizes his emotional reaction to a problem and uses it as a cue to focus attention on the situation producing it, not on denying or avoiding it. Your working out is making it easier for you to do this.

Inhibit your tendency to respond either on the first "impulse" or to do nothing at all. Successful problem solvers are able to "control" themselves so that they do not respond automatically (and usually inappropriately) to problems, or passively avoid them by doing nothing. This is crucial for being an effective problem solver. For example, ineffective problem solvers tend to be impulsive, impatient, and quick to give up if a solution is not immediately apparent. They then become angry and their problem-solving efforts become more ineffective until they eventually diminish completely.

WHEN YOU ENCOUNTER A PROBLEM, TAKE A DEEP BREATH AND SAY TO YOURSELF: "STOP AND THINK."

S.O.L.V.E. Your Problems

You will now learn a technique that will help you create new solutions to *any* kind of problem you encounter. The technique has two major goals. First, to *involve* you in the skills that will make available to you the *greatest* variety of potentially effective responses for dealing with the situation. The second goal is to *increase* the probability that you will select the best response from your various options. To help you remember the technique, remember the acronym S.O.L.V.E. It stands for:

S   State your problem
O   Outline your response
L   List your alternatives
V   Visualize your consequences
E   Evaluate your results

State your problem

The first thing to do in problem solving is to *define* and *identify* the problem situations in your life. People normally experience problems in areas such as work, finance, health, social relationships, and family life. Thinking about each of these aspects of your life will help you identify the area in which you operate least effectively and have the most problems. This is the area you will focus on as you develop your problem-solving skills.

Outline your response

The second stage of problem solving is to *specifically* and *comprehensively* describe the problem and your usual response.

The need for specificity and comprehensiveness in describing the details of your problem cannot be overstated. You must avoid the use of terms that are too vague or ambiguous to be meaningful; consider *all* the available facts and information and, if necessary, seek additional information not immediately available. When you state a problem specifically and concretely, you "force" yourself to make relevant what may have seemed at first glance to be irrelevant. This is another way the work-out process gets you to make use of all available facts (i.e., maximum cognitive engagement).

WORK-OUT NOTE

Research has demonstrated that effective problem solvers typically translate abstract terms into concrete examples, whereas poor problem solvers typically make no such translation. But one cannot deal directly with an array of facts. By formulating the various issues reflected in the details of the situation, the direction of the problem-solving process becomes more clearly focused.

Answering these questions will help you make the problem specific:

- Who is involved?
- What happens or doesn't happen that bothers you?
- When does it happen?
- Why does it happen?
- How does it happen?

Focusing on these points will help you specify your typical response in terms of what you do or don't do:

- How you do it
- How you feel
- Why you do it
- What you want

After you have defined your problem in detail, you can begin looking at it in different ways. The technique to use is "reframing," changing your perception of the situation so that you can generate novel responses. You can reframe *any* problem by thinking about the following:

The real problem isn't who is involved;
the real problem is where you respond.

The real problem isn't what's done that bothers you;
the real problem is when you respond.

The real problem isn't how it happens;
the real problem is how you feel.

The real problem isn't why it happens;
the real problem is why you respond the way you do.

The real problem isn't the situation;
the real problem is how you respond.

When you reframe your problem, you *shift* the creation of the problem from the situation to you. This gives you the power to deal with the problem by changing *your* response.

Some of the sentences you created by reframing your problem may not make any sense to you. Others may give you penetrating insights for creating an effective solution. *The real problem* is most likely going to be *your response* to the situation that you want to change.

An additional reason for reframing your problem is to help you generate some goals that will contribute to your creating an effective response. As you review your outline, you will see that your goals can change as you begin to reframe your problems.

WORK-OUT NOTE

A good example relating to reframing and problem solving is the famous nine-dot problem. The anger athlete will find out what it is and have fun solving it without getting frustrated.

List your alternatives

The major task during this stage is to generate possible solutions appropriate to the problem situation and to do it in such a way that the most effective response will probably be among those generated. A good problem solver will develop at least half a dozen strategies for accomplishing each goal. The best way to do this is through a process of finding ideas called *brainstorming*. There are four basic rules when you brainstorm:

- Destructive criticism is ruled out. This means that adverse judgments about the idea are deferred to a later decision-making phase. Just write your idea down.
- Freewheeling is welcomed. The wilder the idea, the better. It is easier to tame down than to think up.
- Quantity is wanted. The greater the number of ideas, the greater the likelihood of useful ideas. Don't stop until your list is good and long.
- Combination and improvement are sought.

Review your list and see how some of your ideas can be turned into better ideas, or how two or more ideas can be joined into still another idea. Use productive criticism.

At this point, your brainstorming should be geared to formulating general strategies for solution achievement. You need a good plan first. Leave the details for later.

W O R K - O U T   N O T E

Underlying these brainstorming processes are two basic principles of idea production. They are *deferment of judgment* and *quantity breeds quality*. Both principles are validated by research.

STICK TO DEVELOPING YOUR STRATEGIES BECAUSE THE LAST ONE MAY BE THE BEST.

Visualize the consequences

Now that you have several different goals, each with strategies for implementing solutions, you are ready to "visualize" the consequences so that you can select the best solution. Some people do this quickly and automatically. Others are slow and make an effort to consciously anticipate what consequences will result. Whether you are "automatic" or deliberate, this part of the problem-solving process will be most helpful to you when you do it thoroughly, rigorously, and consciously. Here's how:

- Go over your strategies to your goals, crossing out each one that is clearly ineffective. Be on the lookout for combining one into several.
- Next, write down your three best strategies. Under each one, list any positive and negative consequences that might result. Helpful questions to ask yourself are: How would this strategy affect what I feel, need, want? How would it affect people in my life? What are its short-term and long-term consequences? Visualize yourself dealing with the different outcomes.
- Choose the strategy that has the best consequences.

W O R K - O U T   N O T E

Good problem solvers believe that long-term positive consequences are better than short-term positive consequences, and solutions that better a relationship will be more lasting than those that benefit only you.

Evaluate your results

You are now at a point in the problem-solving process where you have analyzed the demands of the situation, generated the various courses of action, and made a decision on the basis of your rating of the consequences.

The final stage is the hardest because you now have to *act.* You have a new response to an old situation. It is time to turn your decisions into actions.

After you have tried your new response several times, observe the *actual* consequences. Are they happening as you thought? Are the consequences meeting your goal? Is this solution actually better than the old solution?

If not, use problem solving to develop alternative strategies. You may also want to repeat other parts of the problem-solving process. The anger athlete does this until he has found a productive solution.

Problems are a fact of life. It is in your best interest to learn how to work them out. You will be a much happier person!

TAKE ACTION

Use S.O.L.V.E. to help you with a current problem.

STATE YOUR PROBLEM

_____

_____

OUTLINE YOUR RESPONSE

_____

_____

LIST YOUR ALTERNATIVES

_____

_____

_____

_____

VISUALIZE THE CONSEQUENCES

Strategy 1:_____

Positive Consequences	Negative Consequences
_____	_____
_____	_____
_____	_____
_____	_____

Strategy 2:_____

Positive Consequences	Negative Consequences
_____	_____
_____	_____
_____	_____
_____	_____

Strategy 3:_____

Positive Consequences	*Negative Consequences*
_____	_____
_____	_____
_____	_____
_____	_____
_____	_____

Implement the strategy with the best consequences.

EVALUATE RESULTS

Satisfactory_____ Why?_____

Unsatisfactory (start over)_____ Why?_____

THE BIGGEST MISTAKE PEOPLE MAKE
IN THIS WORK-OUT IS

to let themselves be overwhelmed by the rigor of the S.O.L.V.E. technique. They ask, "Do I really have to do all of this?" The answer is YES—the first time. You've been stuck in a problem situation, and your old habitual solutions are not working. You need to follow each step of the model so that you can clearly identify goals and achieve them. As you become more skilled at problem solving, you can tailor the procedures to your style and much of it will become automatic. You can prevent yourself from becoming overwhelmed by focusing on one part of the problem-solving procedure at a time.

WORK-OUT NOTES

_____

_____

_____

_____

_____

_____

_____

_____

_____

_____

_____

The Anger Library

> *Recommended for:*
> 1. *People who are chronically angry*
> 2. *People who want to eat well*
> 3. *People who want to add more mileage to their lives*
> 4. *People who need a good laugh*
> 5. *People who want to enjoy life more*

PURPOSE

Malnutrition, lack of exericse, and a poor sense of humor will put a chip on your shoulder. The anger library offers you a collection of material that will help you control these factors and convert them into powerful interventions that will increase your ability to manage your anger. You're not expected to use the whole library at once, so browse through it and take out the work of your choice.

INFORMATION

Anger Attrition Through Nutrition

Nutrition affects how you manage your anger in more ways than you think. For example, when you confront an anger-arousing situation, your muscles become tense, producing a high level of lactic acid. If your diet is deficient in milk or leafy vegetables, you may not have enough calcium to buffer the lactic acid, making it harder for you to effectively relax to counteract the anger arousal. Inappropriate eating habits also figure in high blood pressure, obesity, irritability, headaches, fatigue, and poor self-esteem—all symptoms that not only increase your proneness to needless anger but also make it more difficult for you to manage your anger. Simply stated, malnutrition is a nutrient of anger. Here are some things you can do to get anger attrition through nutrition:

Eat a variety of foods. Eating a variety of foods is the best way to assure that you get the forty to sixty nutrients you need to stay healthy. Include foods each day from each of these major groups:

> vegetables and fruits
> bread, cereal, and grain products
> milk, cheese, yogurt
> meat, poultry, fish, eggs, beans, peas

Avoid fats. The average American gets 45 percent of calories from fat whereas a nutritious eating style should give you only about 30 percent of your calories from fat.

Eat more whole foods. Examples of complex carbohydrates that are good for nutrition are raw or lightly steamed vegetables, fruits, whole grains and cereals, brown rice, beans, and seeds.

Avoid sodium. Sodium is an essential nutrient but Americans tend to consume ten times more than they need.

Eat frequent, calm meals. It is generally thought that four or five small meals a day are better than two or three large meals, especially if you experience a lot of stress.

When you are angry, instead of eating, write your angry feelings down, do something constructively physical, express your feelings to the person you are angry with, or share them with a friend.

Eat slowly. It takes approximately fifteen to twenty minutes after food reaches your stomach for your brain to get the message that food has been eaten. Structuring your meals to last for at least twenty minutes will give you the feeling of being full after eating a reasonable amount of food.

Ex-er-cis-ing Out Anger

Vigorous physical exercise effectively works out anger because it provides a natural outlet for anger arousal and the daily muscular tension your body builds. It also gives you practice in the skill of converting physical arousal into energy for productive action, making it easier to convert anger arousal into energy when you are angry.

There are two major rules for choosing and implementing exercise:

RULE 1: Make sure you like the exercise.
RULE 2: Be consistent.

Honoring Rule 1 will make it a lot easier to honor Rule 2.

One type of exercise that honors both rules, that is easily available to you, is brisk walking. It may well be the one activity that will produce the most benefit for the greatest number of people. Chances are you will find yourself having less inertia for starting a walking program than any other kind of exercise. Here is a procedure to follow for implementing a walking program:

- For five minutes, walk at a vigorous pace. Take your pulse *immediately*. If it is approximately *50 percent* of the maximum heart rate for your age group, go on to the next step. If your pulse is *already above the 70 percent level,* continue to walk at this pace *every other day* until it *falls below* that level. Then proceed. (You can calculate your maximum heart rate by subtracting your age from 220. Then multiply the resultant number by the percentage indicated in each step.)
- For five minutes, walk at a vigorous pace. Take your pulse immediately. If your pulse falls below the 70 percent level, then proceed with more action. If your pulse is over the 70 percent maximum, continue at this pace. Take five-minute walks every other day until your pulse falls below the 70 percent level. Then take more action.
- Alternate one minute of slow jogging with one minute of brisk walking for five minutes. Take your pulse immediately. If it is above the 70 percent of the maximum heart rate for your age group, continue to alternate one minute of jogging with one minute of brisk walking every other day until it falls below that level. When you get to that point, you can proceed on your own. Gradually, you will end up spending more time jogging or even running in order to stay at the 70 percent maximum heart rate. It is good policy to continue jogging until you feel winded. Then slow down to a brisk walk for a minute. If you *can't* carry on a conversation while you're jogging, you are going too fast. *Check* your pulse frequently until you find a pace that will keep

your pulse at about the 70 percent maximum heart rate for at least twenty minutes. Then you're on your own.

• Take a cool-down period to gradually restore you to your physical equilibrium. Always finish your exercise sessions with five minutes of slow walking. Take long steps and let your arms hang loose and shake your hands. Rotate your head around on your neck a few times in one direction and then in the other direction.

After you start a walking program, it will be easier for you to start other exercise programs.

WORK-OUT NOTE

An important benefit of exercises is that they heighten your awareness of what physiological arousal "feels" like. Getting this feeling makes it easier for you to increase your sensitivity to the fact that you are becoming anger aroused.

Laughing More

How many laughs do you think you have a day? If it's under fifteen (three of which should be belly laughs) classify yourself as an underlaughed individual. A good sense of humor makes you laugh more and be angry less. Laughing helps you work out anger because *the physiological arousal* it produces is antagonistic to anger arousal. When you laugh, you release the physical and mental tension that is leading you toward anger or is maintaining your anger. For at least a moment, you can forget about your troubles. But that moment gives you the *time* to reappraise the situation more productively—and in a better mood! Try to be angry and laugh at the same time—you'll find it's impossible to maintain a sullen mood when laughing out *loud*.

WORK-OUT NOTE

Besides helping you work out anger, laughing has a positive effect on your general health. A popular example is the case of Norman Cousins, former editor of *Saturday Review*. Suffering from a disease diagnosed by physicians as incurable, he unreeled *Candid Camera* episodes and Marx Brothers films and, in part, belly-laughed himself into the pink. His anecdotal account of his self-styled healing became a best-selling book and many people have looked upon that successful personal experiment as the kickoff in the game of humor-as-Hippocrates. On a more scientific note, recent and encouraging evidence suggests that humor may directly attack the pain associated with inflammatory conditions such as arthritis, gout, and those resulting from certain injuries. Mirth and laughter stimulate the brain to produce catecholamines—the alertness hormones, including epinephrine, norepinephrine, and dopamine, which prepare us to respond physically for either fight or flight. The arousal hormones in turn stimulate release of endorphins. As the level of endorphins in the brain increases, the perception of pain decreases. Laughter, then, causes our bodies to produce our own painkillers. It has also been shown that the increased level of catecholamines in the blood can reduce inflammation.

The best way to increase your laughter is to develop your sense of humor. Your sense of humor is not innate. You can learn to be funny. Here are some ways to get some more laughs and help you develop your humor skills.

- Put on your *Candid Camera* glasses. This is easy, fun, and loaded with "Ha-ha/aha" moments. Take ten minutes or so out of your day, distancing yourself from your home and office environment, and pretend it's a *Candid Camera* episode and you're the Camera. Look around you, observe all the silly, goofy, and therefore very human activities going on that just ten minutes before seemed so damn serious, earthshaking, and stomach churning. This can be a terrifically lightening and enlightening experience.

PUT ON YOUR *CANDID CAMERA* GLASSES
WHILE YOU DO YOUR WALKING

- Humor meditation. For five or ten minutes or whatever amount of time you can spare during the tensest part of your day, stop and take a humor-meditation break. During this meditation, shut out the outside world and read a funny passage from a jokebook or from a humor scrapbook or think of a past funny experience

- Create a humorous environment. Create a humor-filled environment by setting up a bulletin board in your room or office that has on it cartoons, funny photographs, jokes, and humorous quotes.
- Exaggeration. Exaggeration is one of the most important and versatile humor skills that you can have in your repertoire. It quickly puts things in perspective while making a point. You can develop and practice your exaggeration muscles by connecting similes to smiles. You can make this connection by using the following structure to create exaggerated similes:

(subject) is as (adjective) as (exaggerated simile).

Example: Our town is so small that the 7-Eleven closes at ten.

Playfulness

Playfulness is a crucial humor skill that can be learned and practiced. Being playful with words, images, associations, and situations can be of great help if you are serious about nurturing your sense of humor. Playfulness is an important attribute in developing funnies spontaneously. It also helps in developing flexible thinking. Puns, rhymes, exaggerated funny images are all good ways to be playful.

Perhaps the most important thing to remember about humor is to look at it, and expect it. If you do, you'll probably see its laughing face everywhere, even smirking from behind the things that make you angry. Enjoy!

TAKE ACTION

1. For five days, monitor how many servings you have of each of the major food categories. For each category, divide the total servings by five to get your daily average for the five-day period. Then compare your eating pattern to the ideal to see if you need more or less.

	Day 1	Day 2	Day 3	Day 4	Day 5	Ideal Serving
MEAT, POULTRY, FISH, AND EGGS						
serving = 3 oz. lean meat 2 eggs						2
BREAD AND CEREALS						
serving = 1 slice bread ¾ cup cereal						4
MILK, CHEESE, AND YOGURT						
serving = 1 cup milk 1 medium slice cheese						2–4
VEGETABLES AND FRUITS						
serving = ½ cup 1 apple, 1 orange 1 medium potato						4
FATS AND SWEETS						
serving = 1 candy bar 2 tbs. salad dressing 1 cup ice cream						0
CAFFEINE						
serving = 1 cup coffee or black tea						0
ALCOHOL						
serving = 1 beer 1 glass of wine						0-1

2. List an exercise you would enjoy doing and that is available to you and implement it in your weekly schedule.

   Exercise_____   When you will do it_____

3. Think of at least two things you can do that will help you stick to your exercise program. Useful examples are doing it with a friend and setting exercise goals.

4. Develop two ways to exercise at your job or in other restricted areas. Useful examples are walking up the stairs, walking around the corridor or room, parking further from your destination and walking, and body twists.

5. Each day ask your lover or children if they have heard any funnies.

6. Practice playfulness by playing daily with a play sheet. Write your name or concept and list all the associations, words, and images that come to mind, forgetting logical sense.

PLAY SHEET

*NAME OR CONCEPT*_____

_____

_____

_____

_____

_____

_____

THE BIGGEST MISTAKE PEOPLE MAKE
IN THIS WORK-OUT IS

to visit their anger library but not take anything out.

W O R K - O U T   N O T E S

_____

_____

_____

_____

_____

_____

_____

_____

_____

_____

ANGER WORK-OUT #15

Lovers and Others

> *Recommended for:*
> 1. *People who have an angry, irritable, and high-strung mate*
> 2. *People who want to improve their relationships*
> 3. *People who enjoy helping others*

PURPOSE

The "Me Decade" emphasized taking care of ourselves. But if you want a loving relationship, you're going to have to learn to take care of others, to help them handle their emotions and feelings, particularly anger. Unfortunately, few individuals know how to help their mates deal with this complex emotion. Consider the following statements that therapists and good friends hear, far too often:

"I can't stand it when she gets like this."
"I'm afraid. I never know when he will explode."
"I feel so helpless. I know he's angry and I can't help him."

When persons close to you cannot handle their anger, it creates many problems. Distress is added to *their* lives, interfering with performance and potential. Their work and personal relationships suffer, increasing their anger. Not knowing how to work out, they take it out on you. And what about the times *you* actually do something that provokes them? You will probably be abused verbally (and possibly physically) or given the cold shoulder for some time. Eventually, the relationship becomes characterized by the anger affect. It seems that not a day goes by without a scream or a sulk. Arguments are the norm. A loving relationship becomes inpossible. Living with someone unable to handle anger is difficult, if not unbearable.

When you can help your lover and others work out their anger, you make *their* lives more productive, and you communicate to them that you are sensitive to their needs and feelings. When your lover and others perceive you as genuinely caring about them, a loving relationship can evolve.

Anger Work-out #15 will help you help your lover and others work out *their* anger, especially when it is directed at you.

INFORMATION

Listening to Anger

The biggest obstacle to overcome in helping your lover work out anger is being able to listen to it.

Listening to someone's anger, especially when directed at you, is very difficult. It can really affect you deeply. Why? We all have our own reasons, and many people don't really know why, only that they react with defensiveness and anger. Let's examine some of the common reasons that may contribute to such a response.

One reason you may react with angry, defensive behavior is that you think the person is trying to tell you something about you through their anger. Imagine that you are talking with your wife or lover and complete the following sentence: "When you tell me you are angry at me, you really mean _____." Frequent responses are: "I'm stupid." "You want me to leave." "You think I owe you an apology." "It's my fault."

The fact is, when most people pointedly tell you they are feeling angry, they do *not* mean anything else. It just means they feel angry. Nine times out of ten, it is usually you, the listener, who attributes another meaning to the anger.

If you always assume that people are trying to tell you something else when they express anger, communication becomes very difficult. It suggests that you never trust that people are honest with you. Anger is anger. When you accept it and work it out, it will pass. If you fight it ineffectively, it will become chronic.

COMBATING MIND READING WILL HELP YOU
LISTEN TO ANGER.

Some people respond with anger to their mate's anger because they view each argument as a win-or-lose situation. This leads to a power struggle and anger becomes a way to defend their self-esteem from giving in, from losing.

The work-out process is based on the belief that viewing arguments as a right-or-wrong situation is detrimental to both parties. Nobody likes being wrong, or losing, and it is too stressful always to have to win, to be right. In any argument, both people are usually a little right and a little wrong. The work-out process takes the position that people argue not because one is right and the other is wrong but because people differ in their appraisals. The mistake that most couples make is in thinking that being different is bad, and each tries to force the other to see it as they see it. This perpetuates arguing and intensifies anger.

Being different is not bad. It's just different. Difference is what gives the world color and contrast. In fact, research has shown that while similarities are important in initiating a relationship, it is differences that help sustain them by creating interests and growth. You could never live with someone who is exactly like you.

AVOIDING THE RIGHT/WRONG ISSUE WILL MAKE IT EASIER FOR YOU TO LISTEN TO YOUR LOVER'S ANGER.

We also react angrily when someone expresses anger at us because we may not like hearing what is being said about us. Do you like to be reminded of your shortcomings?

When your lover gets angry at you or points out something about you not to his or her liking, it is often a part of you that you don't like either. These are "hot spots." We get angry because we perceive the comment as being threatening and would rather ignore it than confront it. And we deflect the anger back at them because we are being forced to acknowledge our flaws.

W O R K - O U T   N O T E

One reason we don't want to confront our hot spots is that we frequently feel helpless to do anything about them. In this context, anger feels better than helplessness. The paradox, of course, is that responding with destructive anger keeps us feeling helpless.

How can you learn to listen to anger so it doesn't escalate into a full-blown explosion? Here are a few techniques:

- The next time your lover gets angry at you, be aware of how long you can listen to him without getting angry. Challenge yourself to increase this time each time he expresses anger at you. You will find that it becomes easier and easier to listen to his anger.
- When your lover is expressing anger at you, take a deep breath—and another. Count to five to yourself while inhaling. Count to five to yourself while exhaling. This will help

you relax and make it easier for you to listen.

- If you begin to feel angry, take a time-out. After your time-out, come back and listen again.

Responding to Anger

What can you do in the midst of a barrage of anger directed at you? How can you respond to make the exchange productive?

You have already taken the first step by learning how to control your anger and becoming more aware of your own feelings. This prevents escalation of the situation and *increases your listening receptivity*. Given the fact that you do listen, here are some specific ways that you can respond that will help your lover work out.

Reduce her anger arousal

Reducing your lover's anger arousal will prevent *her* from escalating and experiencing intense anger arousal. This helps your lover avoid the anger trap and keep things "cognitively" in perspective (the same effect it has for you). The best way to reduce your lover's anger arousal is *not* to tell her to "relax" or calm down—this will tend to increase her anger arousal—but rather, for *you* to *do* something that will relax her. The following actions may be effective:

- Getting her to sit down or stop her present activity
- Offering her a drink of water or a noncaffeinated drink
- Moving from the anger environment into another environment (kitchen into living room)
- Suggesting a ten-minute time-out

All of these responses are based on the strategy of getting your lover to *slow down* her response (and thereby *reduce* her anger arousal) without telling her. It is very important to remember that your lover's responses are not something you can control. Therefore, it is quite possible that she rejects your attempts to calm her; the point, however, is that you still have options in how you respond. Your constant effort to relax her will reflect your helping intent.

Hear your lover

Listening to anger is much more than sitting down, being patient, and letting your lover blow off steam. Listening means making a concentrated effort to understand what your lover is angry about. Learning to listen is a skill that takes *time* and *practice* to develop, but here are some specifics that will help you get started.

- Do not interrupt. Interruption escalates the situation. It communicates that you are not listening. If you have the urge to interrupt, take a deep breath and remind yourself "to listen."
- Be aware of your body language. Good eye contact and body posture are nonverbal signals that you are listening.
- Summarize in your own words what you think your lover is saying. Be sure to acknowledge your lover's "right" to feel the way he does. *Ask* if you have captured the message.
- If your lover says you don't understand, explain that you want to. *Ask* for some examples that will help clarify the issues. Make sure you take responsibility for not understanding. Saying "You don't make sense" will only escalate the situation or cause him to withdraw and create the anger affect.
- If your lover says you do understand, ask what can be done to resolve the situation. *Agree* to a solution only if you can implement it. Otherwise, the provocation will repeat itself, triggering more intense anger because you didn't follow through. When this happens, your mate loses confidence in you and says things like "You always say you'll change, but you never do."
- If you disagree with your lover, it is still important to remember to *validate* his feelings. Responding with "You shouldn't feel that way" inevitably creates a power struggle that escalates the current "problem," and in the long run, contributes to the anger affect. The best strategy is to help your lover (and yourself) clarify expectations, and counterpunch any cognitive distortions. Then focus on a solution that *benefits* the relationship, as opposed to benefiting only one of you.

WORK-OUT NOTE

When you focus on the relationship, you end up meeting your needs and those of your lover. When individuals focus on their own needs, they may feel good, but their relationship may suffer. A good example is the man who says: "After twenty years of marriage, she wants a divorce. I thought our marriage was great." For him it was; for her it wasn't. When you have a good relationship, the needs of both of you are met.

Change your behavior

This is the hardest part of responding to your lover's anger because it means confronting the fact that the only way to remove the provocation is for *you* to change. In other words, you acknowledge that you are doing something provoking. Whether it's keeping the house clean, paying more attention, or being nicer to the in-laws, this calls for you to *do* something differently. Here are two strategies that you can use to make change easier for you and your lover.

Establish the desired behavior in small steps. This prevents the pressure of having to change all at once.

Example: Keeping the house cleaner the way you said you would.

> For the first week, focus on keeping the kitchen cleaner.
> The next week, add keeping the bathroom clean.
> The next week, add keeping the living room clean.
> Keep adding steps till the provoking behavior is resolved.

As you master each step, you gain confidence that you can change and progress to the next step. At the same time, your lover sees that you are in *fact* changing.

Involve your lover in the process by mutually monitoring your behavior. Every week, you and your lover need to sit down and graph the progress you are making (or not making). To make this procedure effective, it is essential that you have (in advance) specific examples of what good behavior looks like.

Example: Paying more attention to spouse.

> Verbal compliments when appropriate
> Doing activities together
> Asking mate how her day was

The graphing of your behavioral changes helps change the cognitive appraisals that your lover makes, which are reinforced by the positive benefits she is receiving.

As you change your behavior, you will begin to experience a tremendous reward: Your lover will express less anger at you and be more productive because anger is being worked out.

Helping Lovers and Others Work Out

Many times, your lover, friends, or kids will be angry about things that have nothing to do with you. In these cases you can help them work out by taking several actions.

Recognize low levels of anger

The better you become at recognizing a low level of anger, the easier it becomes for you to help them work out. This is because you can intervene during the early stages of distress and help them before they get caught in the anger trap or begin to feel their situation is hopeless.

Most people only recognize others' *high* level of anger. One reason is that we misinterpret low levels of anger as not really being anger. We think others are merely annoyed or irritated, but annoyance and irritation can escalate into full-blown anger. And even low levels of anger cause unhappiness.

A good way to recognize a low level of anger is to pay attention to the words used. Work-out experts agree that words used to describe anger correspond to the levels of anger experienced. Here are some examples:

Anger Level

Low	Medium	High
(1-2-3)	(4-5-6)	(7-8-9-10)
bugged	angry	enraged
irritated	mad	furious
bothered	upset	livid
annoyed	pissed	

VOICE VOLUME INCREASES AS THE ANGER LEVEL
INCREASES.

W O R K - O U T   N O T E

Tuning in to the words your lover uses to express low levels of anger will also help you become sensitive to the words *you* use for your own levels of anger. This gives you another *cue* that it's time to take action.

**KNOWING YOUR MATE'S ANGER LEVEL INCREASES
YOUR EMPATHY AND ABILITY TO HELP HIM OR HER.**

Communicate that you want to help

As soon as you recognize that your lover is angry, *verbally* communicate your desire to help. This can be accomplished by responding in a way that invites your lover to share his feeling with you. These types of responses "open the door" for your lover by signaling that you are willing to listen and help. Here are some examples of door openers:

Would you like to talk about it?
I would like to help you.
Tell me about it.
You can talk to me if you like.

Help them problem-solve

As you listen to others and begin to grasp the nature of their anger, you can begin to help them work out by using their problem-solving skills. Anger Work-out #13 will help you do this well, but as a start follow these conversational guidelines.

- Avoid displays of impatience. This will demonstrate your willingness to help and give you the time you need to accurately hear the anger.
- Avoid blaming them for the "problem."
- Avoid ridicule for getting angry over "such a little thing."
- Express open-mindedness, even toward irrational ideas.
- Make sympathetic remarks when appropriate.

Following these suggestions increases others' willingness to share their feelings with you because they see you are listening. They see that you care and become receptive to your input. Help them by getting them to focus on accurately appraising their anger. When it's needless and unjust, simply talking about it will tend to dissolve it because you can help them clarify their cognitive distortions. When it's just, focus on helping them work it out by developing productive actions.

More important than the specific strategies discussed, helping your lover or others work out their anger requires an attitude that implies willingness to give emotional support. People who give such support to their lovers usually find it is reciprocated. In this sense, the best way to look out for number one is to look out for number two!

WORK-OUT NOTE

Sometimes others will not let you help them. If this happens, you can help by *letting* them work out on their own. Offer support when and if requested.

TAKE ACTION

1. List two things that make your lover angry at you. Then give yourself practice in listening to your lover's anger by visualizing and hearing him expressing his anger at you. See yourself listening to him without getting defensive or angry. See yourself responding productively. Visualize and hear this scene for five minutes a day, for one week.

   _____

   _____

2. List two things that you can do to relax your lover when she is angry at you.

   _____

   _____

3. Begin to pay attention to the words that your lover and others use to describe their anger levels. Do the same for yourself.

4. List three door openers you can use with your mate when you recognize that she is angry.

   _____

   _____

   _____

THE BIGGEST MISTAKE PEOPLE MAKE
IN THIS WORK-OUT IS

to try to work out their lovers' anger by telling them they are overreacting or that things are OK. This either escalates the situation or causes them to withdraw because they think you don't take their needs into consideration or that you don't understand them. They feel alone too. You can avoid this mistake by helping them work out their anger instead of telling them not to be angry.

WORK-OUT NOTES

_____

_____

_____

_____

_____

_____

_____

_____

_____

_____

_____

ANGER WORK-OUT #16

Forward Pass

Recommended for:
1. *People who can't let go of the past*
2. *People who are constantly unhappy*
3. *People who have self-defeating behavior*
4. *People who want to move forward*

PURPOSE

All of us remember incidents that still make us angry. But there is a sharp difference between those incidents that merely irritated us and those incidents that caused tremendous anger when they occurred. As time passes, remembrance of the minor incidents loses capacity to rouse us to anger.

More serious provocations affect us differently. They may have occurred decades ago, but although the song may be over, the melody lingers on. The major provocation might have been a single event, or a series of events that was so arousing and overwhelming that we weren't able to cope. Instead of working out our anger, we covered it up so that what we have is the equivalent of a deep infection incompletely covered by a scab permitting the pus to spill out occasionally. For example, the spouse who is still angry about being rejected in early marriage has little chance to experience a happy marital relationship because past anger still smolders. Anger at divorced parents may persist from childhood days and prevent a warm loving relationship with either or both parents.

Anger Work-out #16 will provide a means for making past anger pass so that you can go on with living, loving, and learning.

INFORMATION

When Anger's Lasting

Passing anger means time in itself is only a Band Aid of relief. *Action* is required—you make the anger pass by taking an active role, by working out.

The best way to do this is to deal with the *feelings* the anger creates, not the anger itself. When you focus solely on the anger ("It makes me so angry every time I think about it"), you relive the provocation *emotionally* and open the wound. The infection spreads. Dealing with the feelings gives you the chance to discover what is wrong and get them better. Healing the wound is the goal of passing anger.

Not all of us have anger to pass, and not everyone recognizes past anger. Here are some signs that indicate that past anger is still lasting:

- Feeling unappreciated and unloved
- Physical ailments like stomachaches, migraine headaches
- Hesitancy to call your parents
- Bickering with your spouse
- Feeling you want to "get back" at your boss
- Feeling incomplete
- Decreasing sexual vitality
- Eating binges and other self-destructive behavior
- Having grudges and resenting people or what they do

These types of feelings and behaviors are the manifestations of unresolved anger. They come from a variety of anger experiences all sharing a common theme: They *hurt* you. Working out your hurt feelings is the key to passing anger and preventing it from becoming everlasting.

Getting in the Passing Lane

If you have signs of past anger, your next step is to acknowledge the hurt feelings you didn't express in the past and the specific situations that created them. This requires courage on your part, but until you work out your past anger, every other positive health strategy you attempt will be severely undermined. Acknowledging past hurt can be accomplished by completing the sentence:

I feel hurt when _____ and I am still hurting. Nine times out of ten, the part you complete will be an anger-provoking experience. But rather than focus on the anger experience per se, focus on letting yourself acknowledge the hurt. If you are doing Anger Work-out #7, you can probably handle it.

For most people, following these instructions is more anxiety arousing than anger arousing because they have to acknowledge the hurt they felt, yet denied. What you are feeling now is normal. If you feel like crying, by all means do so. It will help you relax and deal with the task at hand. Ask yourself, "What prevented me from expressing how I feel?"

Usually the answer is "I was afraid." But afraid of what? Probably of being rejected. The truth is, while you may not have said anything, you still expressed your anger and hurt in self-defeating ways as previously noted. Year after year, your resentments mounted until at last, you have a *false intimate relationship*—you want to feel close, but don't. People in false intimate relationships usually act happy but they really aren't. Working out past anger offers the opportunity to change a false intimate relationship into an intimate one.

By acknowledging your past hurtful feelings, you put yourself in the passing lane. You may already feel a bit better.

W O R K - O U T   N O T E

> The assumption that your negative feelings may threaten your relationship is based on a cognitive distortion that it is inappropriate to express anger to someone you love or who loves you. A more accurate cognition is that it is inappropriate *not* to express how you feel to someone you love or who loves you.

Getting Support

The next step in making past anger pass is to get support for your feelings. Ask an "A" team member who is not involved with your past anger to help you. Read each one of your hurt statements. After each statement, have the other person say, "I understand; that's OK." Instruct him *not* to make any value judgments or attempts to change your feelings. His job is to support your right to feel. Believing that you didn't have this right is one of the reasons you passed over your hurt in the first place.

By getting support for your feelings, you develop confidence for dealing with them. Instead of being frightened or ashamed by them, you feel entitled to them. Having your feelings supported makes you feel good.

Insight into Hindsight

This step gives you the opportunity to safely share with the person involved the feelings you never expressed, and to develop insight into the feelings of those who have hurt and angered you. These are important elements in working out past anger because they draw attention to the fact that sometimes our feelings and actions are based on how we think someone else feels (mind reading). Knowing how they feel helps us understand how we *affected* them and why they did what they did. Many people are astonished to find out that people provoked them or hurt them because the other people perceived that they were being hurt or provoked. For example, in many marriages, each spouse holds back love for fear of being rejected by the other. They hurt each other and are angered by the other for the same reason. Many find this to be the case *after* their marriage. There are two effective ways to get insight into hindsight: 1) using the hot seat and 2) getting a witness.

The hot seat

- Arrange two chairs facing each other.
- Sit in the chair of your choice, calling it number one.
- Breathe slowly and deeply until you are relaxed.
- Visualize the target of your anger sitting in the other chair.
- Vocalize your past hurt, and whatever else you feel, to the image: "I feel _____" (this must be done out *loud*), and emphasize why you are talking to the other person.
- Be specific in your dialogue, and speak in complete and direct sentences.
- After you finish, stay seated to think and feel.
- Change seats. Visualize yourself in the other chair as you think the other person sees you. Express how you think he or she feels. As you finish, stay seated to think and feel.
- Keep changing seats as "each" of you expresses himself. You will eventually feel as though you have said what you wanted. By playing the other person, you have probably gained some insight into how the anger and hurtful experience affected him or her. Don't be surprised to learn that you were not the only angry and hurt person.

Most people think this exercise is silly, but it will actually make you feel better. If you do feel silly doing it, find a picture of the person who hurt you and "talk to it." Again, the essential point is that you must talk out loud.

USE A TAPE RECORDER SO YOU CAN HEAR WHAT YOU ARE FEELING.

Before going on, it is important to do one more thing. Relive a joyful experience you had with the target of your anger. Do it with energy so that you will be reminded that the reason you hurt so much is because the other person was so meaningful to you. Getting in touch with love helps heal your wound and takes some of the poison out of the relationship.

W O R K - O U T   N O T E

It is important to talk out loud because it desensitizes you to the fear of expressing past anger and hurt. Since you are only "role playing," you are safe to express how you feel. There is no threat. This experience is for you and is not necessarily to be shared—or acted upon—with the people involved.

Getting a witness

Another way to increase your understanding of your past anger is to get witnesses who actually observed your anger experience or hurt. Ask them how they perceived the situation and how they think you responded. Their perceptions may give you penetrating insights into the distortions that keep your hurt and anger alive. Many times, their perception of the situation will be so different from yours that you will reappraise the situation more realistically, which will help you pass anger. If your feelings are validated by the witness, you can seek relief in knowing that your feelings are justified. Talking to your brothers and sisters about how your parents treated you and asking for their feedback is making use of witnesses. Parents who ask their grown children how they "saw things way back when" are also making use of the witness principle.

Writing It Off

Since our anger and hurt occurred in the unchangeable past, we tend to feel helpless to do something about it, which increases resentment. You need to *do* something, and writing a letter may meet this need.

WORK-OUT NOTE

> Many people don't write a letter because they reason that they can do the same thing in their minds. These people mistakenly believe that the sole purpose of writing a letter is to clarify and acknowledge their feelings, positive and negative. The work-out process emphasizes the *action* of writing a letter on the basis that the *act* of writing in itself will reduce your past (or present) anger because it serves as a productive outlet for your "stored up" anger arousal and gives you a sense of power. (Most work-out experts miss this point by focusing only on the content of the letter.)

It is a good policy to reread your letter as a reminder that you *did* do something about it, and continue writing letters until you lose the need to do something. You will then feel much better because you have "written it off."

Having a Peace Talk

This optional step involves meeting with the target of your past anger and expressing your desire to improve the relationship. For some, this is the most important part of releasing anger, especially if the person involved is intimately related, as a lover or family member.

If you use this step, remember that the goal is to heal the wound, not to reopen it. Here is how to make a peace talk make peace:

- Make sure you are alone with the person and will not be interrupted.
- Emphasize how important this meeting is for you and that you are doing it because you care.
- Express how you felt at the time of the incident and why you felt that way. Then talk about your feelings as they are now.
- Express positive feelings, if any—a peace talk is warm.
- Focus on what you want to happen.
- Ask for the other person's feelings—then and now.
- Hug and cry if you feel like it.

Having a peace talk is an emotional experience. Tears at the beginning reflect your hurt and bitterness. As you move through it, the pain begins to lift. Now tears reflect the joy of making peace and hugging feels great.

Getting Closure

Closing the door on past anger is the final stage. Closure means that you no longer let past anger and hurt sabotage your current life. You have "let go."

Closure may be a very long process, and many people aren't able to let go. Their anger is everlasting. Nobody knows exactly how to ensure success in letting go but the preceding steps will help you approach it.

Getting closure has occurred if you honestly do not feel hurt about the past. When you let go, you are ready to live again.

W O R K - O U T   N O T E

What about past anger experiences like being raped, or molested, or being the victim of a drunken driver or a disease? The anger and the hurt experienced from these events will probably never go away. But that does not mean you should wallow in your hurt and self-pity. Trying to pass the anger is still your best option.

TAKE ACTION

1. List any symptoms that may reflect past anger.

   _____

   _____

   _____

2. Complete the following sentence:

   I felt hurt when_____

   and I am still hurting.

3. I write down what prevented me from expressing how I felt.

   _____

   _____

4. Ask somebody you trust to listen to your hurt feelings.

5. Write a letter to the person provoking you. Write anything you want, but you will be most helped by writing how you felt at the time of the anger and how you feel now. Do not mail your letter.

6. Have a peace talk if necessary.

7. Work out until you can honestly say, "I no longer feel hurt or angry about this."

8. Repeat this procedure for all the hurts you have.

THE BIGGEST MISTAKE PEOPLE MAKE
IN THIS WORK-OUT IS

to tell themselves and others they have passed the anger and hurt when they really haven't. Their current relationships continue to be infected by their old wounds. Acknowledging that your anger has not passed may be painful, but at least it gives you the *chance* to work out. It will not pass on its own.

W O R K - O U T   N O T E S

_____

_____

_____

_____

_____

_____

_____

_____

_____

_____

ANGER WORK-OUT #17
Family Feud

Recommended for:
1. *People whose children have emotional problems*
2. *People who are angry at their parents*
3. *People who want to help their kids grow*
4. *People who want to improve their relationships with their parents*

PURPOSE

Getting angry at your parents or kids may lead to lack of contact with them, but it can *never end* the relationship. These relationships are permanent. You may choose to disinherit a son, but he is still your child. And the anger created by avoiding contact with family members usually is more damaging than the conflict that started it all.

Anger Work-out #17 helps you work out anger in your closest blood relationships by getting you to take action in two ways:

- As a parent: to teach your children how to work out their anger in general, i.e., anger that does not involve the parent as the object.
- Between a parent and child: to work out the anger that exists between you.

INFORMATION

Becoming a Helpful Parent

Helping your children work out their anger provides a valuable skill for your child and is a proper function for you as a parent. Unfortunately, most parents don't know how to help their kids work out.

W O R K - O U T   N O T E

Children and adolescents who can't work out anger are prone to many disruptive behaviors such as fighting, lying, stealing, cutting school and dropping out of school, and drug abuse. Also, research indicates that a child's inability to work out anger may lead to a personality prone to coronary and other health problems. It seems that parents who can help their children work out their anger will also help them live longer.

How helping parents view anger

Seeing a child get angry is a frightening and frustrating experience for parents, regardless of the child's age.

Thinking it is totally unacceptable, we try to deny it and soften it:

"He never acts that way" (3-year-old son).
"I don't know what got into her" (30-year-old daughter).

We try to control it:

"Stop acting like that or you'll have to go upstairs."

We get angered by it:

"I said stop it!"

These responses certainly don't help and may make matters worse.

Helping parents handle children's anger differently because they view anger differently. Here is their VIEW:

V. They *validate* a child's right to get angry by encouraging emotional expression. They want their children not to fear their emotions and to be able to express their feelings, to know that their feelings count, and that all feelings are OK to have, even anger and hate. Here are some ways to validate children's feelings:

- Label a feeling for a child—"You seem to be angry" (as the child is yelling or pouting), "and that's OK."
- Talk about the children's feelings in front of them to a significant other—"Josh is really angry" (mother to father).
- Hold or touch children when they express their feelings, or when they are obviously disturbed but not verbalizing their feelings.

VALIDATE YOUR CHILD'S FEELINGS BY ALLOWING THEM TO BE EXPRESSED.

I. Helping parents *investigate* their children's anger. They use it as a cue that the child is hurting or experiencing some other distressful feeling. This requires that you be sensitive and aware of what's going on in their lives. The more you tune in to your children, the easier it becomes to recognize when they are stuffing their feelings or about to explode. Ask yourself:

- How do I know they're angry?
- What is making them angry?
- How come it makes them angry?

Tuning in to your children also helps them feel secure and provides them with the emotional climate that encourages the expression of their feelings. Investigating feelings validates them.

E. Helping parents teach their children to *express* anger productively. Acknowledging and validating the right to get angry is one thing; expressing it productively is another. Two things parents can do to facilitate productive anger expression are setting limits and encouraging self-disclosure.

Setting Limits. The goal of setting anger limits is to allow the child to get angry and let him express it in a way that is not self-defeating and hurtful to others. If you are like most parents, your limits focus on telling your child how he *cannot* express anger, rather than how he *can* express it.

Setting limits is not: "You can't get angry; you shouldn't feel like that" (invalidates the anger and provides no outlet).

Setting limits is: "Sit down and tell me about it without yelling and screaming" (validates anger and provides outlet).

Here are some guidelines for setting limits:

- Set limits early, even as early as six months of age.
- Be consistent. When helping parents mean NO, they say it every time they see their child testing the limit inappropriately. They don't give mixed messages that breed confusion, constant testing, and undesirable behavior.
- State the limit and the reason for it. Even when their kids are toddlers, helping parents use reason with them.
- Do not threaten. Make sure that the consequences for violating limits *relates* to the limit in question (make the punishment fit the crime, in other words). "You missed curfew; now no allowance" is not as effective as "You missed curfew; you can't go out."

Many times, your children will test your limits by making overt challenges. Helping parents know that the child has a need to be autonomous. In this context, testing limits is not necessarily a sign of disobedience. Helping parents go by this rule:

> If the child tests the limit in an inappropriate manner, they continue to enforce the limit. When the child tests the limit appropriately, they consider revising the limit. As an example, instead of breaking her curfew, a sixteen-year-old girl sits down with her parents and discusses whether or not she can stay out later. Because of her mature discussion, her parents consider revising the limits.

Self Disclosure. Helping parents encourage their children to talk about their feelings by teaching self-disclosure. As children learn to self-disclose, they become less likely to stuff their anger because they do not fear their feelings. Learning to "talk their feelings through" decreases the chances that they will escalate their anger. Strategies that will help develop the self-disclosure process include:

- Do things together with your kids. *Time* together creates opportunities to self-disclose.
- Ask your kids what they want to talk about. Don't ignore their interests.
- Talk at bedtime. Read or tell stories, and have your child tell the story. Ask for his feelings. Structure other "talking times," too.
- Encourage forms of self-expression: drawing, dancing, playing music.
- Ask your kids for their opinions and discuss them.

- Use nonverbal behavior such as head nodding to encourage their talking.
- Do not put down what they feel.
- Model self-disclosure to your children by using I-feel-emotion statements.
- Do not interrupt them.
- Thank your kids for sharing their feelings with you.

When children learn to self-disclose, they become spontaneous and emotionally confident. They feel comfortable talking about their feelings, and because they've had limits, they express their feelings appropriately, productively, and creatively.

W. Children learn how to *work out* their anger by being taught the concepts that underlie life-support skills. Helping parents want their children to be competent people. (Adapt concepts to the child's age so that the child can "work out" automatically on his own.)

Options and choices

When children learn to think in terms of having options and choices, they lower their risk of getting frustrated or angry when their wants are blocked because they have learned to generate alternative responses. Furthermore, the fact that they can make a choice reduces feelings of helplessness and creates a sense of confidence.

Consequences

Children need to be taught responsibility for their actions. They should be able to recognize, anticipate, and evaluate the consequences of their behavior. Parents can help by:

- Stating the consequence of the child's behavior for the child.
- Asking hypothetical questions involving moral dilemmas and focusing on the consequences of the child's response.
- Using natural consequences. Letting the children experience the natural consequences of their behavior, even when it may be adverse. "Saving" your kids too many times prevents learning.

Teaching consequences helps children understand how their behavior affects the world and their *responsibility* for the results. They are quick to learn that escalating anger is not productive.

WORK-OUT NOTE

Setting limits is different from teaching consequences in that it restricts the child's behavior by defining boundaries. With consequences you point out what *will happen* if the child acts a certain way and let him experience his results if he *chooses* to do the behavior. Teaching consequences illustrates how to make operant learning work for you.

Goals

Parents need to encourage their kids to have goals—goals for the moment and for the future. When a child thinks in terms of goals, he is considering the consequences of his behavior and evaluating whether his actions will help achieve his goals. Thinking of goals makes it easier for the child to *direct* his energy for productive results.

Interpersonal interaction

Helping parents teach children that they don't live in a world of "me." They want children to know that their behavior has an effect on others and that how they treat others will affect how others treat them. They teach their kids three essential rules for resolving interpersonal conflict.

- What did I do?
- It takes time to think.
- Put yourself in the other guy's shoes.

None of these lessons comes naturally to kids, but those who learn these rules are found to be less impulsive and more adept at solving interpersonal problems.

Alternatives, consequences, goals, interaction: These are some of the concepts that helping parents teach their children. They are interrelated and develop skills (problem solving, decision making, value clarification) that make it easier for children to become competent people, enabling them to work out their anger.

Summary: Helping kids work out

V. Validate children's anger.
I. Investigate their anger.
E. Encourage expression.
W. Help them to help themselves work out.

**HELPING YOUR CHILDREN WORK OUT THEIR ANGER
HELPS YOU WORK OUT YOUR ANGER.**

Cleansing the Blood Line

One source of anger that exists between parent and child is the parent's need to control the child. Giving up the need to control is the basis for working out the anger that exists between you and your child, and between you and your parents. This is accomplished by resolving the parental paradox.

WORK-OUT NOTE

Obviously, there are many things that create anger between parent and child. However, clinical research points to the fact that the most intense conflicts between parent and child, and those that create the most damage to the relationship, center around the parent's need to control their child and the child's need to break loose without losing parental support.

The parental paradox

Parents have a need and an obligation to do their best in raising their children. When the parents are doing their job, they are in the paradoxical position of preparing someone they love to leave them eventually.

As the child prepares to leave, the parents' own emotional needs are aroused, making it difficult for them to "let go" of their child. Leaving inevitably creates parental feelings of anger, hurt, and frequently depression. Letting go of a child is hard.

Many parents avoid these feelings by not helping the child as much as they could when the child's need to be autonomous is at its *strongest*. At this time, parents try to exert control by trying to "run their kids' lives"—which confuses the child and inhibits his decision making—or, they *withdraw* their necessary support just when the child needs it most. Either response prevents the child from feeling emotionally confident and making a decision. In a sense, the parents "hold on" by keeping their child a "child."

Such responses are deleterious for three reasons. First, the child resents the parent for making him so dependent. Self-esteem is lowered as the child is led to believe he cannot function on his own. This in turn provokes the anger of the parent who gives the child the contradictory message, "You should be on your own, but you aren't able to be." The child then gets more angry at his parents.

Second, by keeping children dependent, the parents come to realize that they have not fulfilled their parental obligation. They then feel frustrated, guilty, and angry.

Third, the daily relationship becomes a constant power struggle as the parents' need to hold on conflicts with the child's need to go. You hear things like:

"Don't tell me what to do."
"You're making a mistake. Listen to me."
"So do what you want. . . ."

The more the child resists, the more the parent attempts to control, either directly, or indirectly by withdrawing love and support. A natural relationship becomes painful.

Parents can save themselves and their children a lot of anger and grief if they learn how to let go of their children in a way that meets the emotional needs of both sides.

WORK-OUT NOTE

The specific stage at which the parent exerts control or withdraws support is irrelevant since the child is continuously striving for autonomy. It is the parents' parental style that is the problem. For example, when their children are toddlers, they tell them how to play with their toys; when they are college bound, they tell them what school to go to or "I won't pay for it"; when they are adults, they tell them what house to buy or "Don't come to me when it doesn't work out." This parental style is the complete opposite of that of a helping parent and stems from the parents' need to control their child. When the child refuses to do what the parents want, the primary parental response is anger. Think about how you respond when your kids don't do what you want.

Letting go

What makes it especially hard for parents to let go is the fear that their children will abandon them as soon as they are able to stand on their own feet. For many parents this fear is a reality, but it becomes understandable once you examine how they try to control the relationship.

Parents who have healthy separations *trust their kids to succeed*. They consistently provide their children with an emotionally secure environment so that as the child grows, they feel emotionally confident in the decisions the child makes and the child knows that he can depend on his parents for appropriate support. These parents act on the belief that if they help their child grow, the child will *always* see them as nurturing and will *always* want to return (i.e., visit home, consult on important decisions). When parents trust their children to succeed, they give them an implicit vote of confidence that they are competent.

Trusting the child to succeed is the way to integrate the parents' own dependency needs with the child's need to be independent. The best way to trust your child to succeed is to become a helping parent. The best way to help your parents trust *you* to succeed is to *make them feel secure* in their relationship with you (consequently, they will lose their need to tell you what to do because you keep them connected to you in more productive ways).

The more secure you and your parents feel with each other, the less you threaten each other. It becomes much easier to work out your anger.

W O R K - O U T   N O T E

A frightfully familiar scenario is the parent who says that every time he trusts his kid to succeed, the kid "screws up." Therefore, he has to tell his kid what to do. Parents like this fail to confront the fact that they teach the children to "screw up" as a way to hold on to them. Clinically, one might say that they sabotage their children's development to meet their own needs.

Becoming a helping parent, and making *your* parents feel secure: When you can do *both* you can work out the anger that's all in the family!

TAKE ACTION

1. Ask your children daily how they are feeling.
2. List two things that provoke your children and next to each write down a strategy that will help them work out their anger the next time they confront the provocation.

Provocation	*Work-out Strategy*

3. List one thing that you can do the next time your child gets angry to validate his feelings.

_____

4. List one limit that you have set for your children regarding their anger and monitor yourself to see whether you consistently enforce it.

_____

5. List one thing you can do to encourage your child to self-disclose.

_____

6. List one thing you can do that will help teach your children the consequences of their behavior.

_____

7. Help your child set a goal.

8. List one way you can teach your kids that how they treat others affects how others treat them.

_____

9. List two things you can do to make your parents feel secure about your relationship.

_____

_____

THE BIGGEST MISTAKE PEOPLE MAKE
IN THIS WORK-OUT IS

to hold on to their fear that they will be left alone when their child grows up. Research shows that helping parents are rewarded by having children who show them love forever.

W O R K - O U T   N O T E S

_____

_____

_____

_____

_____

_____

_____

_____

_____

_____

ANGER WORK-OUT #18

The Anger Work-out at Work

Recommended for:
1. *People who get angry at work*
2. *People who want to go up the organization*

PURPOSE

It's a well-known fact that being able to handle anger on the job is a decisive factor in whether or not we go up or out of the organization. Consider the following:

- A study conducted by the Center for Creative Leadership in Greensboro, North Carolina, concluded that a major reason executives are derailed—successful people who were expected to go even higher in their organization but are fired or forced to retire—is their inability to handle anger, especially under pressure.
- Charles Collins, former president of Fairchild Republic and executive vice president of Fairchild Industries, attributes the worst mistake of his thirty-six-year career to getting angry: "I had made a mistake. I got mad and didn't organize for the problem. . . . I was hot." Soon after, Edward G. Uhl, Fairchild's president, removed Collins and named a new president to the aircraft company.

- New York Yankee Cliff Johnson's inability to control his anger resulted in a fight with teammate Goose Gossage. Johnson was promptly traded. (Gossage has since left the Yankees too. His salary demands probably angered the team's owner.)
- Research compiled by *Fortune* magazine indicated that the employees of the toughest bosses in America have to deal with their bosses' fits of anger, which typically leads to low productivity.
- Many of the most distinguished CEOs, such as Reginald H. Jones (General Electric), Walter B. Wriston (Citicorp), and Thomas J. Watson, Jr. (IBM), all acknowledged that the skillful management of anger was crucial to individual and organizational effectiveness. Their views are now research-validated.

There is no doubt about it. Inability to handle anger on the job is a sure way to derail yourself off the track of success. Anger Work-out #18 will help you work out your anger by showing you how to put anger *into* your job to make it better for all. Specifically, you will be armed with some hands-on proven work-out strategies for dealing with the five most common anger provocations that come with *any* job.

INFORMATION

Three Essential Job Skills

Each of the provocations in this work-out is unique and therefore requires a different work-out strategy. However, the anger athlete inplements each of the following concepts for every job provocation.

Manage the anger arousal immediately

Showing inappropriate emotional arousal on the job is undesirable, especially if you are not the boss. It makes you look out of control, and it impedes your peak performance. Convert anger arousal to energy by directing it into job activities to get your work done. If you are too angry to sit down and be "creative," then use your anger arousal to do your busy work so at least you are getting something accomplished. This helps you feel productive and gives you a sense of control, so that you can "go back" and productively confront the source of your anger. If you have a Relaxation Response (see Anger Work-out #9), use it.

Acknowledge that you are choosing to keep your job

Common comments that people make to themselves when angry on the job are "That's the way it is." "There's nothing I can do about it." "I have to accept it." "It's not that terrible." These are very powerful anger-management statements in the job setting. Although they help you initially to release your anger, they do not help you work out because they also imply that you are helpless, which paradoxically increases the anger you wish to reduce. Chronic anger may result. The work-out process uses the assumption that you don't have to accept "it," but rather that you *want* to because you want to keep your job. Acknowledging that you want to keep your job allows you to get angry and yet keep things in perspective as coming with the territory. "I don't like it, but I will learn to deal with it" is much more productive than "Nothing I can do about it; it's not that bad." The latter statement denies the anger where the former is task oriented: "Given the fact that I'm angry and I want to keep my job, what can I do about it so it doesn't happen again?" This attitude provides the impetus for turning your arousal into energy so that you can develop a work-out strategy.

Implement action

Being action oriented means you expect that in most cases the provocation will not resolve itself. Action is required that is based on a plan to resolve the provocation and prevent recurrence. By being action oriented, *you* take the responsibility for working out the provocation.

When Your Anger Ruins Your Job

This section will give you practice in dealing with job provocations by exposing you to the five most common anger-provoking situations associated with employment. Thinking about a work-out strategy for each one helps you develop the skill of using anger strategically.

WORK - OUT NOTE

The provocations described are based on data collected from more than thirty-five hundred individuals who completed the anger work-out inventory or have participated in anger work-out seminars, workships or classes, as well as nonseminar/workshop participants who also completed the anger work-out inventory. The provocations are found to be common to all job environments, whether it's in a *Fortune* 500, government-agency, small-business, or institutional setting, and are categorized as being either abusive or unjust or both. More important, they reflect accurate perceptions of the reality of the situation. Thus they cannot be dealt with simply by using anger-management coping statements or having realistic expectations (although it helps). They require hands-on strategies.

Provocation #1: Being left out. "I can't stand the way they ignore me."

Although we may try to shine as individuals, our job involves other people. It's a group effort for most of us. But it's awfully hard to join the group if the group doesn't want you. Being left out at work, or not being accepted by your peers, is anger provoking on two accounts: 1) It prevents us from doing our job most effectively, and 2) it threatens our need to belong. Feelings of hurt are also experienced. What would you do?

Provocation #2: The critical boss. "He's constantly putting me down, rarely telling me what I do right. I feel he doesn't appreciate me. I get angry just thinking about him."

Having a critical boss is infuriating because it means being subjected daily to destructive criticism. It is unjust and we feel abused. Responding with anger is the typical response, but because the job environment inhibits expressing anger toward our boss, we stuff it and become angrier. We tend to get back at our boss by taking a passive-aggressive stance. We do everything the job dictates, but *not* one iota more. We take out our anger by withholding enthusiasm, imagination, and support. These actions, however, give the boss further reason to criticize. What would you do?

Provocation #3: Not getting the promotion you deserve. "I busted my butt. I deserve that promotion."

Here are some popular ways of dealing with this provocation.

- Stew and complain to your friends.
- Let everyone know you were robbed.
- Berate yourself.

Most people choose all three ways of responding with little to show for it except feelings of resentment, jealousy, and perhaps a lost job. What would you do?

Provocation #4: Being maligned by co-workers. "When I heard what was being said about me, I went through the roof. I almost decided to quit."

Being victimized by false rumors is a consistent anger arouser. It is abusive and unjust. And the rumors frequently cause irrevocable damage. Anger is justified. What would you do?

Provocation #5: Dealing with the incompetent boss. "That guy's stupid and incompetent."

By far and away, the most common and most anger-provoking situation is having to deal with the incompetent boss. His incompetency blocks your need for fulfilled work, and hampers the work of your organization.

How to Put Anger into Your Job to Improve Your Job

Here are some proven hands-on work-out strategies for the preceding provocations. Pay attention to how the goals produce the strategies.

Provocation #1: Being left out

Goal: To break into the group and achieve group acceptance.
Work-out strategy: First examine your own behavior to see if you are precipitating your own rejection. For example, if your job peers are frequently talking about people and places that are foreign to you, sitting back silently and uncomfortably will most likely be seen by them as aloofness. Or if you are always talking about things you do that exclude them, you may come across as a snob, or as someone who doesn't want to join the group. There are two actions for you to take.

1. *Verbally emphasize* the important experiences you share with them. If, for example, a nurse is being left out by the other nurses on her floor, she can assimilate herself into their group by emphasizing common nursing-school and

job experiences. Shared experiences foster cohesiveness. This is in sharp contrast to complaining to the supervisor that nobody likes you, or angrily telling individual members that you don't like the way they treat you. The latter tactics will only make the group more resistant to accepting you.

2. *Make a direct effort to join the group. Be friendly.* If the group is going out to lunch, for example, you needn't wait to be asked. You can take the initiative and say, "Mind if I come along today?" Even if the entire group doesn't welcome you, perhaps there are one or two people who will accept you.

If you are pleasant, helpful, friendly, and the group still shuts you out, it may be a warning that the group itself is in trouble. Perhaps the department is underequipped or understaffed; that may lead to pressure, tension, and anger. Maybe the manager or the members of the group are "stuck," caught in dead-end jobs with little prospect of advancement. These situations breed anxiety, jealousy, friction, and gossip. The "stuck" group tends to become a clique, loyal to its members, hostile to outsiders. They substitute social satisfaction for the job opportunities they don't have and define success as belonging to the clique; they may exercise their only power by keeping you out or keeping you down by refusing to share information or expertise. This may be the time to make a lateral move, transferring to another department, or to get out.

WORK-OUT NOTE

Breaking into a group does not always involve emphasizing common experiences or being friendly. There are many creative ways to do it. Jane Pauley, correspondent of *The Today Show*, tells how she integrated herself into her work group.

"Geography counts in the workplace. I used to have an office that was tucked around the corner out of the way. It was the only one of the twenty offices where people felt obliged to knock. Recently, when another office became available, I moved and it made me approachable. I am part of things now, so people know what's going on inside my office and I know what's going on outside." Today, she's an anger athlete.

Provocation #2: The critical boss

Goal: To make your boss realize that some of his destructive comments are not valid and to alert him to the merits of your work.

Work-out strategy: The plan here is to "structure" the criticism process in a way that will oblige your boss to take a more comprehensive view of your work and thus recognize its overall merit.

Tell your boss that you value his criticisms and ask him if you could meet privately and periodically to review your work. In the first two meetings, he may have a long list of things that you have done wrong, but as the meetings continue, he will begin to note how much you really do accomplish and become aware of his counterproductive habit.

In effect, you work out your anger by helping your boss change his behavior—"forcing" him to stop "pouncing" on isolated errors and instead to judge your competence from a wider perspective. This procedure will become self-perpetuating as he begins to see that productive criticism enhances your work—and his job. On the other side of the coin, by requesting "criticism meetings," you indicate that you are willing and able to accept negative criticism in a productive way. This strategy helps you develop a supportive relationship with your boss and makes your job a little easier and a whole lot more enjoyable.

Provocation #3: Not getting the promotion you deserve

Goal: To increase your chances of getting the promotion next time around.

Work-out strategy: It's a cliché, but it's true: It's no use crying over spilled milk. Ruminating about how you were cheated isn't going to help you. Nor are you likely to get what you want by threatening to leave (you may, but what happens if your bluff is called?) Use your anger productively by doing the following:

- *Pleasantly* ask your boss why you were passed over, and what you need to do to make yourself the prime candidate for the next suitable opening. Then listen—don't argue or offer excuses. Take notes and state that you will act on what you've been told, and then do so. (This step can be done only if you are managing your anger arousal.)
- Draw your boss's attention to your strong points. Prepare a well-thought-out list of your qualifications. Discuss these points and leave the list with your boss. The next time there is an opening, chances are the boss will be aware of you as a candidate. If you've been tactful and presented a good list, your boss *may* even feel he owes you something right now for having passed over you, and he may give you a raise, a better title, or some other consideration.

• If you are repeatedly passed over for promotions that you deserve, the best way to handle your anger is to channel your energy into your work, improving quality and quantity, making your boss *dependent* on you. Once this is accomplished, you will have leverage to force a promotion. If this fails, stay in your present position and look elsewhere for a position that is worthy of you.

When you follow these steps, you use your anger as a source of positive energy for getting a promotion instead of negative energy that not only makes matters worse but also prevents you from getting the promotion in the future. Acting productively creates a positive attitude. As a result, you feel good.

Provocation #4: Being maligned by co-workers

Goal: To stop current rumors and prevent future ones.

Work-out strategy: You have two choices. First, you can ignore the rumors. This will be an effective strategy if you genuinely do not care what other people think, *and* if the rumors will not affect your job performance, job advancement, and job satisfaction. However, if any of these three job aspects is threatened (which is almost always the case), the second strategy of removing the rumor is more suitable. Here, your objective is to use your anger productively to defend yourself. Here's what to do to remove a rumor:

Trace the Rumor. Ask each person whom he heard it from. Start with the person you heard it from. Before leaving each person, tell him, "I appreciate your not spreading this rumor especially since you now know it's not true. I know that you are not the type of person who would spread a false rumor. *Thank you.*"

Confronting the Rumor. When (and if) you arrive at the source of the rumor:

1. State your feeling. Be sure to use "I" statements and your RR.
2. Attempt to find out what motivated the rumor. Was it something you said or did? Do not argue.
3. Demonstrate understanding and concern by paraphrasing what you heard and restate your feelings.
4. Ask how he would feel if he were in your position.
5. Shake hands and leave on the upbeat.

In the end, people will say what they want to whomever they want. Perhaps your best strategy is to strive for good relationships with everyone.

WORK-OUT NOTE

Sara Weddington, assistant to the president of the United States, illustrates a key aspect of dealing with the rumor starter: "I used to get so angry on hearing that someone said I'd done such and such, when it was 100 percent untrue. On a few occasions, I have confronted the person and said, 'I hear you're saying such and such. I want you to know what the facts are; I know you would not want to spread false rumors.' Maybe that's exactly what they *do* want, but you've got to find them a way out. The old Chinese system of saving face has not gone out of style in the working world." Presidents know the value of working with anger athletes.

Provocation #5: Dealing with the incompetent boss

Goal: To get him to be more competent.

Work-out strategy: You can't fire your boss, so the best plan uses his position to increase success for all. Your specific goal is to minimize any of his detrimental effects and use his job push to implement key projects. One way of doing this is to make your boss an ally so that he will be receptive to your input. Be friendly and show respect. Use a variation of consultive supervision. Ask your boss for his ideas about your work, and in the process educate him. Point out the benefits of implementing certain concepts so that he will use his job power for organizational and individual achievement. Give him plenty of praise when he gives you productive criticism. In time, you will cultivate a productive relationship in which he feels free to ask for your advice. He in turn becomes your champion and helps you develop and advance. In the end, you *may* end up having to deal with an incompetent subordinate—your "boss."

WORK-OUT NOTE

This strategy draws on the assumption that the essence of a superior-subordinate relationship is interdependence. It becomes the subordinate's job to help his superior to do his best job. Japanese management experts know this to be true.

Whether you're a company president or a company clerk, knowing how to handle anger on the job is essential to your job success and job satisfaction. It's a skill that pays well!

TAKE ACTION

1. List two job activities that you can do when you experience anger arousal.

   _____

   _____

2. Make a list of things that either your boss, peers, or subordinates do that provoke you. Then develop a work-out strategy for each one.

Job Provocation	*Work-out Strategy*
_____	_____
_____	_____
_____	_____
_____	_____
_____	_____

THE BIGGEST MISTAKE PEOPLE MAKE
IN THIS WORK-OUT IS

to think it's inappropriate to express anger on the job. This is because they equate anger arousal with expressing anger. This equation binds people to the sweeping generalization that anger on the job can only be counterproductive. Individuals who adhere to this belief are less enthusiastic, less productive, and ineffective. Individuals and organizations that sanction anger expression by channeling anger arousal into creative and productive result-oriented actions are the opposite.

W O R K - O U T   N O T E S

_____

_____

_____

_____

_____

_____

_____

_____

_____

_____

ANGER WORK-OUT #19

Anger and Good Company

PURPOSE

CEO's, presidents, executives, administrators, managers, heads of profit and nonprofit organizations should be aware that any of the following may indicate organizational anger.

- Lowered productivity
- High turnover rate
- Missed deadlines
- Power struggles between employees
- One-upmanship
- Chronic mental and physical health problems among employees
- Lowered morale
- Lack of innovation and creativity
- Unsuccessful turnaround attempts

Organizational anger (OA) sabotoges the effectiveness of your organization by robbing it of energy that it needs to excel.

Anger Work-out #19 will give you techniques for working out organizational anger and in the process, *arouse the positive emotional energy* that is the bottom-line ingredient in achieving excellence.

INFORMATION

Getting Your Company Angry

Organizational anger is negative emotional energy that leads to the signs listed above. It occurs when the organization blocks a significant number of its members from fulfilling their needs. These members then take out their anger on the organization and prevent the organization from functioning satisfactorily. Like an individual, an organization also gets angry when its needs are blocked. Given this set of circumstances, it becomes impossible for members to contribute to their organization and for the organization to help its members. Each "blames" the other for not getting what they want. Organizational anger blocks emotional excellence. Because organizational anger is so prevalent and can develop and spread so quickly, it is essential that you know how to work it out.

W O R K - O U T N O T E

Organizational emotional excellence exists when the individual members and organizations are continually putting positive emotional energy into each other. This leads to better mental and physical health for employees, better job performance, and greater organizational harmony and productivity. More important, it perpetuates the exchange of positive emotional energy between the individuals and the organization. Emotional excellence is the trademark of the ideal organization. Working out organizational anger helps achieve it.

Individuals and Organizations: Who Needs What

All individuals and organizations have certain needs. Organizations whose members have a good understanding of these needs and know that individual needs are *compatible* with organizational needs are in a good position to prevent organizational anger from ruining them.

Defining a need

Needs can be thought of as a source of energy that presses you to fulfill unfulfilled conditions, physical or psychic urges.

Individual and organizational needs are related in a hierarchy, or an ascending scale of importance. Unmet basic needs claim priority, and other individual and organizational needs must be postponed. Blocking fulfillment of these other needs leads to anger.

Individuals and organizations may be visualized as pyramids with the most essential needs at the base; the needs closer to the peak of the pyramid have to await fulfillment of the more basic needs.

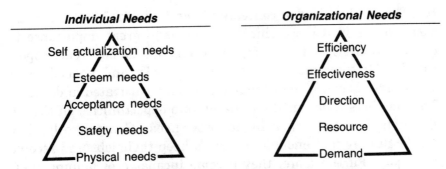

Here is a brief description of the corresponding needs individuals and organizations seek to fulfill. Failure to satisfy these needs leads to anger.

Individual Needs	**Organizational Needs**
	Level I.
Physical Needs	**Demand**
Your physical needs are the most primitive and basic and include such things as food, water, air, and sleep. They must be satisfied if life is to be sustained. They are also the easiest needs to satisfy.	The most basic of an organization's needs is a demand for the product or service it markets.
	Level II.
Safety Needs	**Resource**
Safety and security are necessary to protect physical needs and are reflected in insistance on fair treatment, job tenure, job protection, and insurance.	The organization's second most basic need is for resources to fulfill the demand for its product or service. Lack of necessary resources threatens the organization's survival.
	Level III.
Acceptance Needs	**Direction**
One of our strongest needs is for social acceptance, for belonging, for association, for friendship and love.	All organizations have, either stated or implied, a purpose for their existence. That purpose must have dynamic direction, be able to respond to changes in supply and demand.

Esteem Needs
Self-esteem requires subjective and objective recognition that one is a worthwhile person making a reasonably significant contribution.

Level IV
Effective
Organizations need to be effective, to show results, to use resources to meet demand.

Self-Actualization Needs
Self-actualization means reaching our full potential. The struggle to satisfy more basic needs such as acceptance and self-esteem directs energy away from self-actualization and may lead to frustration.

Level V.
Efficiency
The final need of any organization is efficiency. Efficiency relates not to results but to how well an organization achieves its results. Only after satisfying most of its other needs can an organization focus on satisfying its need for efficiency.

The implications of conceptualizing individual and organizational needs in a hierarchical manner is of great importance to organizations. Specifically, organizations that do not create opportunities for their members to meet levels IV and V needs hurt themselves because their members become frustrated and angry. The members then put their energy into opportunities off the job that help them meet their higher-order needs. Consequently, they put forth only just enough energy to keep their jobs and receive their pay. Furthermore, they become incapable of helping their organization meet its needs. In short, the organization loses its members' positive emotional energy. Instead, organizational anger is born.

How the Healthy Get Wealthy

Integrating individual and organizational needs works out organizational anger and lays the groundwork for emotional excellence. Here's a detailed plan for how the healthy get wealthy.

Integrating Need #1: Physical needs and the need for Demand

The most basic needs for the individual are biological or physical. Survival requires fulfillment of these needs and is dependent on earnings. An organization's survival is dependent upon demand for its product or service. Thus, a demand for the organization's product or service permits survival of the organization and allows the individuals employed to meet their physical needs.

An increasing demand for organizational products or services may require the individual to work overtime. Reduced demand requires adjustments that could include layoffs. The organization meets the needs both of its members and itself by maintaining demand for its product or service. It becomes management's responsibility to revise its product and service offerings on a continuous basis so as to match current and anticipated demand. *Only* by fulfilling this responsibility can the organization's continuance, including its ability to provide employment to its members, be assured.

W O R K - O U T   N O T E

A good example of a company's failing to integrate Need #1 is Atari, the video-game giant. The past management's inability to keep its product in demand led to a plant shutdown ousting over four hundred employees. The organizational anger this created has probably been a key reason that has so far prevented the company from regaining its dominant position. It will be interesting to see how its new management works out.

Integrating Need #2: Safety Needs and the need for Resources

The individual's second basic need is for security and safety. The organization's second basic need is to fill the demand for its product or services. By providing its members with survival and security, the organization helps direct the energy of its members to satisfy demand for the organization's product. Interdependence and integration of organization and individual is demonstrated. "Productivity through the people" results.

Richer organizations are not necessarily able to satisfy the security needs of their members better than the less-endowed organization. The individual need for security extends to having reasonable predictability of surroundings, enabling the person to be free of anxiety and to feel at ease. In contrast, inconsistency in management, poor communication and a policy of ignoring the worker, favoritism, or discrimination can create anger among the organization's members. Enlightened organizations recognize these potential sources of individual frustration and try to avoid such problems.

WORK-OUT NOTE

Hewlett-Packard illustrates how an organization *can* provide security for its employees despite external conditions. In the 1940s, HP decided not to be a "hire and fire" company. This policy was demonstrated during the 1970 recession. Instead of laying people off, HP asked everyone to take a 20 percent cut in pay as well as to work 20 percent fewer hours (the same applied to the heads of the company). This helped the organization meet its needs during the recession *and* provide security and survival for its members. Another example: The three-billion-dollar corporation Dana has written into its statement of company philosophy: "It is essential to provide job security for our people." Contrast this with Atari, or with what an executive at Avon says, "Morale at Avon is terrible. People are scared about keeping their jobs, especially at the top." Excellent companies know the importance of job security.

PROVIDE AND COMMUNICATE SECURITY FOR MEMBERS OF YOUR ORGANIZATION.

Integrating Need # 3: Acceptance Needs and the need for Direction

The individual's need for belonging and the organization's need for direction are integrated by setting individual and organizational goals. Individual goals let the individual see how he or she can help the organization. Group or organizational goals unite the members, creating a cohesive unit and providing direction for the organization. Organizational goals fuse all human resources to achieve excellence.

Remember the following when you set goals:

- Make your goals specific. *What* you want to accomplish and *when* you want it.
- Make your goals big and meaningful. The bigger and more meaningful your goals are to you, the more energy they create for achieving them.
- Believe you can accomplish them. The more you believe you can accomplish your goals, the more energy they create for achieving them.
- Write your goals down. Writing crystalizes thought and thought motivates action.
- Break down your goals into specific steps so that they become manageable.
- Use your goals to lead to other goals. Making each goal a stepping-stone to another goal facilitates progress.

Here are some ways to make organization goal setting effective:

- Make sure the goals are mutually and genuinely agreed upon. This holds true whether it includes the boss-subordinate relationship, or a group of three or more.
- Make your organizational goals comprehensive. Goals should apply to every activity of your organization.
- Apply the strategies for individual goal setting.

MAKE GOALS MEANINGFUL AND BELIEVABLE AND THEY WILL BE ATTAINED.

W O R K - O U T   N O T E

> The chairman of Texas Instruments (Mark Shepherd) affirms the work-out goal procedure: "Teams set their own improvement goals and measure their own progress toward these goals. Time after time, team members set what they feel are challenging but realistic goals for themselves, and once the program gets rolling, they find that they are not only meeting their goals but exceeding their goals. This is something that rarely happens if goals are set *for* the team rather than by the team."

Integrating Need #4: Esteem Needs and the need for Effectiveness

Integrating the individual's need for self-esteem and the organization's need to be effective is dependent on *recognition* and *results*. Individuals want positive recognition and positive attention and organizations want to attain results. By giving individual members and their groups positive recognition you continually improve their results and your organization's results. Excellent organizations attribute their results to their individual members and suborganizations. Letting people know this energizes them to continue their good work. Remember, being recognized reduces anger. Here are some ways to give positive recognition and attention.

- Use "Howdy" rounds. Make contact with each subordinate early each morning to say, "Good morning, what's up?" and again in the afternoon to ask, "How are things going?" Howdy rounds not only help satisfy individual social needs but also help the manager confirm that goals are being met. Using Howdy rounds prevents things from getting out of hand before you become aware of the problem. And by asking nonthreatening questions, you promote communication and interaction.

- Verbally acknowledge someone's good work. Tell a person specifically what he did well and how it helps him and the organization. When possible, turn the verbal praising into a *tangible* acknowledgment such as a letter of commendation, permission to attend a special seminar, or assignment to a project of interest.
- Encourage members to compliment each other's work. This builds morale and group cohesiveness and helps develop friendly competition.
- Develop your own recognition system that singles out individual and group excellence. This becomes a super way not only to build members' self-esteem but also to develop friendly competition.

Integrating Need #5: Self-actualization Needs and the need for Efficiency

Providing an environment that enables the individual to strive for excellence integrates his need for self-fulfillment with the organization's need for efficiency.

Encourage creativity. Here are some ways to increase the creative potential of your organization's members:

- Place a high value on ideas. Ideas crystalize thought. Explain the benefits that can result from a new idea. Possible examples: cost reduction, increased market share, greater job security, problem resolution, new product development.
- Highlight the most challenging areas. Focus on solving key problems and increasing capability in critical areas.
- Demonstrate your willingness to help develop ideas. Be a champion. Being open-minded and flexible are your assets.
- Recognize those who submit successful ideas, and encourage those who are less successful.
- Emphasize personal and organizational benefits repeatedly. Make sure that the benefits are meaningful to the individual.

TRUST YOUR ORGANIZATION'S MEMBERS TO COME UP WITH GOOD IDEAS.

Participative Management Strategies. A second way to integrate higher needs is to use participative management (PM) strategies. These strategies are designed to involve the employee in the processes of the organization. Involvement is both mental and emotional, and encourages the employee to contribute to organizational goals and ideas and share responsibility for their achievement. Although an individual working alone can certainly be creative, the dynamics of group interaction can build enthusiasm for creativity and innovation among a wider range of people within the organization. PM strategies make everyone recognize organizational goals and expectations, and provide feedback related to actual performance versus goals or expectations. They also provide each member with the ideas of all other members and build upon them. This generates excitement and arouses members to find new and better ways to do things. When these resulting ideas are implemented, individual fulfillment and organizational success are affected. Here are some strategies to build participative management.

- Communication meetings. The goal of communication meetings is to keep members informed on what is happening or being planned. The information needs to be communicated in a manner that dispells rumor and speculation while enhancing the credibility of the manager. These meetings should be held periodically at the same time and place, in a setting conducive to communication, and should be brief. Preparation by the manager is key to making such meetings successful. Topics should be work related. The tone of the meetings should remain positive and supportive, and problems should be discussed with confidence that they will be resolved.
- Consultative supervision (CS). This strategy is summed up in four words: "What do you think?" As the name implies, CS means that a manager consults with organizational members in an effort to get the benefit of their ideas *before* a decision is made.

  To be effective, CS requires that the manager generate a receptive climate so that members will feel their input is welcomed. Benefits of CS include better communication, fewer grievances, and less anger. CS can also be done on an informal basis whenever the manager chooses to consult with any or all the members.
- Quality circles (QC). A quality circle is a group of from three to ten people doing similar work under the direction of the same supervisor, who meet for about an hour each week to identify, analyze, and solve problems. Quality circles promote the dignity of organizational members and pride in their roles. There is no guarantee that solutions

reached by group consensus are the best, but QCs build self-esteem and the effectiveness of solutions generated by the group's members. Solutions reached by consensus enjoy greater support than a solution chosen by a manager. A QC can be used effectively as a *group suggestion box* to collect ideas, as a *special project* to deal with temporary or critical organizational issues, and as a *transitional device* in moving toward a more participative management system and culture.

WORK-OUT NOTE

Recent research on quality circles indicates that they often fail because managers and organizations do not remember that each member of an organization sees the organization and other members as they relate to him or her. Individuals are the centers for their own universes, and at best they can be only partially objective. If they perceive that you put the organization above them and feel as though their needs are being blocked, they become demotivated and angry. On the other hand, if you can integrate their needs with the needs of the organization, they will see how their organizational roles can be a productive outlet for their energies and a vehicle for attaining their needs. They will be highly productive and so will your organization.

Getting the Family Feeling

Unfortunately, many heads of organizations and corporations (as well as executives, administrators, and managers) use the team metaphor to build cohesiveness and morale as a means for increasing production. The team metaphor carries with it the dangerous assumption that if you don't "win," you lose. Losing threatens all individual and organizational needs, making it impossible for anybody to feel secure and thus channel their resources into developing the basic needs of an organization. Furthermore, when individuals perceive that their "team" is losing, anger and dissension are quick to surface. Nobody likes to play on a losing team.

The work-out process suggests that the family metaphor is much more appropriate for an organization, because it focuses on helping members satisfy their needs. In return, members value their "family" and maximize their efforts. Excellent companies such as IBM, Delta, HP, Disney all use the family metaphor for this very reason. Increasing productivity is viewed as a developmental process, not a win-lose event. Most important, the team metaphor frequently frustrates individual needs for the sake of the organization while the family metaphor satisfies individual needs by assuming that this will help the family. By focusing on developing members, the family metaphor elicits positive emotional energy, the key to emotional excellence that leads to increasing productivity, quality, and prosperity.

A strategy that develops the family feeling involves *rituals*— events that become ingrained into the organization. Rituals develop the family feeling because they foster cohesiveness despite external conditions (winning or losing is irrelevant). Some common organizational rituals are: announcing and celebrating members' birthdays and other personal occasions, a potluck holiday party, celebrating promotions, a welcoming process for new "family" members, and farewell parties for those who retire or leave.

W O R K - O U T   N O T E

In 1979, the Pittsburgh Pirates all season long used "We Are Family" as their *theme* and team song! That year, they won the World Series.

MAKE YOUR TEAM A FAMILY, THEN YOUR FAMILY A TEAM.

TAKE ACTION

1. Develop a goal that will help you and your organization meet its needs.

   What you want to accomplish:_____

   _____

   When you will accomplish it by:_____

   _____

2. Ask your boss what his expectations are of you and check to see if they are realistic. Take action frequently.
   Sit down with each of your subordinates and communicate your expectations to them. Check to see if they are realistic. Take action frequently.

3. List two tangible things that you can implement to provide recognition.

   _____   _____

4. List two tangible things that you can implement to encourage creative thinking.

   _____   _____

5. When appropriate, conduct a communication meeting to see if there is interest in developing a quality circle.

6. Practice consultative supervision when applicable.

7. List a ritual that you can implement in your specific division, department, etc.

   _____

THE BIGGEST MISTAKE PEOPLE MAKE
IN THIS WORK-OUT IS

also being popularized by current business books—that the organization must meet the needs of its members. This implies that the organization *does* something to its members. This assumption draws on need theory and reflects a major misunderstanding of both theory and research. According to need theory, an individual will inherently strive to fulfill his needs *without* anybody's doing anything to him. Thus, an organization that emphasizes meeting its members' needs misses the boat since the individual will do this on his own. The real question facing an organization is: What do we do (structurally) that *blocks* the members from fulfilling their needs? Removing the blocks frees the positive emotional energy that is inherently part of every individual. This is best reflected in the research that shows that people join a specific organization with the hope that it will let them do what they want, not for what the organization will do for them. This contrasting way of thinking—not blocking needs versus meeting needs—is not subtle and is the key difference between members' feeling as though they work for an organization and feeling as though it is *their* organization. The latter feelings promote excellence in all respects.

W O R K - O U T   N O T E S

_____

_____

_____

_____

_____

_____

_____

_____

_____

_____

_____

ANGER WORK-OUT #20

The X-Rated Work-out

> Recommended for:
> 1. Couples who have poor sex lives and little romance
> 2. People who want greater intimacy
> 3. People who want more sexual energy in their relationships

PURPOSE

"I was so hot, I thought I would explode. I lost control. I can't believe I scratched him. I never acted like that before. I'm so embarrassed."

Does the above statement come from a woman who attacked her husband in a fit of rage, or does it come from a woman who has just made love? Although anger at your lover is certainly not the same as making love, there are striking similarities between anger and sex that can either build or destroy your sexual relationship. Anger Work-out #20 will show you how to turn these similarities into differences, which is the key for keeping anger out of the bedroom.

WORK-OUT NOTE

Fifty percent of couples at one time or another suffer from sexual difficulties. And anger plays no small part. Suppressed anger, or anger that is expressed inappropriately, is a significant cause of sexual problems as well as a primary factor in the loss of sexual feelings between lovers.

INFORMATION

Changing the Anger-Sex Message

The greatest similarity between anger and sex is that, from an early age, we are admonished that it's best not to think, feel, or act angry or sexy. Look at what we are taught:

Anger Message	Sex Message
You shouldn't have angry thoughts.	Erotic thoughts = dirty thoughts =
Forget about it.	wrong thoughts.
Be good and play nice.	Don't touch that part of your body.
Keep it to yourself.	Don't talk about sex.
Don't say anything.	Nice girls don't.

The underlying premise is that it's socially inappropriate to express either one of these feelings. This suppressive attitude is physically, mentally, and socially unhealthy and has the following adverse effects:

We experience destructive feelings such as guilt, shame, embarrassment, and fear for being "normal." Getting angry at your lover over the breakfast table is sure to make you feel bad, sometimes for the entire day. Even thinking angry thoughts can produce feelings of guilt and shame. And if you are like most people, you will have these same feelings for having erotic thoughts about you and your lover, let alone putting them into practice. We feel bad for doing what could make us feel good—regardless of whether we are angry or sexy.

We are not taught how to verbally communicate angry feelings or sexual feelings in a productive way. Most people do not know how to express their anger productively. Similarly, few people feel comfortable telling their lovers they want to make love, or asking them how they can be sexually pleasing, or stating their sexual preferences. Sexual feelings, desires, and preferences are less often communicated directly than by suggestive actions: wearing a sexy negligee, arranging for the children to sleep out, putting your lover's hand on a part of your body that you are embarrassed to describe. Sexual words trigger feelings of anxiety and guilt before they evoke feelings of excitement or pleasure. Suppressive sexual and anger attitudes have created a nation of people who cannot express these feelings productively. Consequently, we become frustrated because we do not know how to communicate our angry and sexual feelings to our lovers.

We are not taught what "to do" when we do express angry or sexual feelings. Besides leaving the room, or sleeping on the other side of the bed, we are taught few options for responding when we are angry. The same is true for sex. People are crippled by anxiety and fear because they do not know what to do when it comes to making love. For example, a man who has not learned how to touch a woman so that she can achieve orgasm comes to view himself as a poor lover, making sex anxiety arousing. And his lover's embarrassment or shame may prevent her from teaching him. Their sex life becomes anger provoking instead of pleasure evoking.

Suppressed anger and sexual attitudes have a paradoxical effect on our sexual relationships. On one hand, they keep us from expressing negative feelings toward our lover on the erroneous assumption that to do so would be inappropriate and threaten the survival of the relationship. On the other hand, they keep us from expressing *positive* feelings toward our lover, which *does* threaten our relationship. Inhibition of sexual feelings then becomes a source of angry feelings, which are also suppressed. If we do express our anger overtly, we yell and scream accusatory statements that further inhibit our sexual feelings. The anger-sex paradox now becomes clear: If you don't get angry, you don't get sexy. And if you do get angry, you don't *want* to get sexy. The first step in working out anger from sex is changing the suppression of these feelings to appropriate and productive expression. Recognizing what feelings you associate with anger and sex, learning how to let your lover know in a clear and accurate manner when you are angry with him and when you are sexually "turned on" by him, and knowing what "to do" when you are angry and when you are "sexy" will do the trick.

The Arousal Dilemma

Anger and sex both lead to physical arousal. The important points here are:

- Anger arousal is a derivative of the instinctual fight-flight response and is thus more ingrained in us than sexual arousal, which we do not experience until the beginning of puberty. (We experience anger arousal at approximately four months old.) This means that it is much *easier* to become anger aroused than sexually aroused and makes anger arousal a more *frequent* response. The frequency and instinctual strength of anger arousal makes it much more difficult for us to suppress than sexual arousal.

- Because of the negative consequences that usually follow anger arousal, and the frequency with which we experience anger arousal toward our lover, we often tend (i.e., are conditioned) to act and think counterproductively when we feel ourselves becoming physically aroused in the presence of our lover, especially in ambiguous situations.
- The initial stages of anger arousal and sexual arousal are identical.

These facts can play havoc with our sexual relationships. Given a (ambiguous) sexually arousing situation (such as watching television together), we "automatically" attribute the early signs of sexual arousal to the more frequent response of anger arousal. We then search our environment for provocations (a sloppy night table, an overweight mate, a big check at the end of dinner) that confirm our right for being angry. Next we begin to *act* angry, which increases anger arousal. The outcome—our anger response is strengthened, our sexual response is further suppressed, and it becomes even more difficult to discriminate between anger and sexual arousal. The process is sure to repeat itself. Now you know why so many potentially romantic and sexual encounters are spoiled at the last minute.

W O R K - O U T   N O T E

> This illustrates a point made in Anger Work-out #1: that sometimes we experience arousal first and then label it as a particular feeling—in less than a second. In this case, we *mislabel* the arousal because of how we have been previously conditioned. It is also a good example of how important it is to be able to accurately use the context of a situation to give feedback about our feelings.

The arousal dilemma is resolved by breaking the negative association of being physically aroused with negative thoughts and feelings so that we can accurately attribute our arousal to the actual (sexual) cause instead of a prefabricated (anger) cause.

This is accomplished by: (1) you and your lover becoming physically aroused *together* by (2) doing *positive activities* in a (3) positive situation. This allows you to feel good when you are becoming aroused *with* your lover.

W O R K - O U T   N O T E

A troubled couple's attempt to improve their relationship by going to the movies or going out for a nice dinner is not necessarily effective because it does not alter the association of negative thoughts with being physically aroused. In contrast, a couple who goes out dancing will feel much better toward each other because they are experiencing positive arousal with each other which will generate positive feelings and positive thoughts, as well as decrease their anxiety the next time they experience physical arousal in a potentially sexually arousing situation.

Your Anger-Sex Vocabulary

Anger-sex words are those words that we use to express both anger and sexual arousal. When we use an anger-sex word, we bond anger and sex and perpetuate the arousal dilemma. Furthermore, because anger arousal is more frequent than sexual arousal, words that would be part of our sexual vocabulary become part of our anger vocabulary, i.e., anger-sex words instead of sex-anger words. Even in sexually arousing situations, anger-sex words tend to elicit some anger arousal. Lovers who use these words mistakenly attribute their "passionate sex" to sexual magnetism when it is really the contribution of anger that makes things extra hot. Unfortunately, these couples continue to use anger-sex words after the sex act is complete.

The suppressive sexual attitude comes into play too. Few of us are taught that it is socially appropriate to use anger-sex words. But because anger arousal is a harder response to suppress than sexual arousal, anger-sex words become more appropriate to say when we lose our temper than when we are sexually aroused. And because of the negative *connotation* that anger-sex words develop, we actively suppress them from our sexual vocabulary. Consider the fact that lovers who report experiencing a lot of anger get *turned off* when their mate says, "I want to fuck you." Also consider that most people say "fuck" when they experience anger arousal, not sexual arousal. Having a small sexual vocabulary makes it even harder to verbally communicate our sexual needs and desires, which prevents us from making our sexual relationship better. In fact, it makes us angrier.

Developing a *separate* anger and sex vocabulary is still another thing we need to do to work out anger from sex.

Separating Anger Communication from Sexual Communication

The fourth similarity between anger and sex is that they both communicate how we feel toward our lover. Anger, of course, projects displeasurable feelings. Couples who fail to separate anger from sex will frequently end up communicating anger *through* sex. They develop one of the following anger-sex styles:

W O R K - O U T   N O T E

An important point is that couples can use any of the anger-sex styles *without* being cognizant of their anger. As applied here, acknowledging anger toward our lover is anxiety arousing for most of us. Therefore, it is better to be "unaware of it." This reflects the point made in Anger Work-out #1: Cognitive does not imply having an immediate awareness. Use the *quality* of your sexual relationship as a cue to alert you to possible anger between you and your lover.

Sexually unresponsive. You may choose not to have sex or become a "willing" but unresponsive lover. Although this hurts your lover, it prevents you from meeting your own sexual needs. The sexual frustration increases your anger toward each other. Using this anger-sex style makes sex a source of anger as well as a means to communicate anger.

Sexually aggressive. Where else but in the bedroom can you scratch your lover's back, pull his or her hair, yell abusive anger-sex words, have it accepted, and end up feeling good? This anger-sex style changes the *context* of the anger by giving permission to act out anger actions after an argument under the guise of "making up." Conflict resolution is short term (as long as the sex act) and intimacy is superficial since these couples will still feel they can't communicate.

The affair. Sex is a poor weapon. Communicating your anger by having an affair hurts your lover but the anger it provokes in him or her is usually so intense that it causes irrevocable damage to your relationship.

Couples who constantly use these anger-sex styles perpetuate the integration of anger and sex. It becomes impossible for them to develop a loving relationship because they are never expressing positive and negative feelings in a clear, accurate, and appropriate manner. Their mixed messages breed confusion, making honesty and intimacy rare and trust nonexistent. They bring anger into their bedrooms.

Couples who have learned to separate anger from sex don't use anger-sex styles. They have learned to work out their anger in a way that lays the groundwork for having a loving relationship. As they express negatives appropriately, so they express positives. When they have sex, they enjoy a love-sex style— positives are communicated through a positive act. They become turned on not by a reservoir of stuffed anger but by the prospect of developing their relationship. These are the couples who keep anger out of the bedroom.

WORK-OUT NOTE

When couples can work out anger from sex, they energize their relationship. Working out enables them to express positive feelings through observable positive actions, not intentions. The positives they express to each other let both partners feel that they are committed to the relationship. They continue to work out together.

TAKE ACTION

1. Put an A (anger) and an S (sex) next to the feelings you associate with anger/or sex, and then discuss these feelings that you associate with both sex and anger with your lover.

Guilt	_____	Good	_____	Dirty	_____
Embarrassment	_____	Nervous	_____	Bad	_____
Shame	_____	Hurt	_____	Powerful	_____
Fear	_____	Cold	_____	Relaxed	_____
Anxiety	_____	Rejection	_____	Evil	_____
Pain	_____	Pleasure	_____	Uncomfortable	_____
Other	_____		_____		_____

2. Complete these sentences and show them to your lover. He or she will be very appreciative.

I am angry at you when:

_____

_____

_____

I am sexually turned on by you when:

_____

_____

_____

3. List two productive things your lover can do to let you know she is angry at you. Ask her to do the same.

_____

_____

Lover's response

_____

_____

List two pleasurable things your lover can do when you are making love. Ask her to do the same.

_____

_____

Lover's response

_____

_____

4. List two positive activities that you and your lover will enjoy doing together and that will be physically arousing, and build one of these activities into your weekly schedule. Repetition is essential.

_____

_____

5. List the words that you use when you are experiencing either anger arousal or sexual arousal toward your lover. The words you list for both are your anger-sex words.

Anger Arousal	*Sexual Arousal*
_____	_____
_____	_____
_____	_____
_____	_____
_____	_____

6. List the words or phrases that you and your lover will use to express angry and sexual feelings toward each other. Be sure that each word or phrase occurs on only one list.

Anger Vocabulary	*Sex Vocabulary*
_____	_____
_____	_____
_____	_____
_____	_____

7. List two ways that you can communicate positive feelings in a clear, direct, and appropriate manner.

_____

_____

8. Think of your sex relationship. If it matches an anger-sex style, look for a way to work out anger toward your lover.

THE BIGGEST MISTAKE PEOPLE MAKE
IN THIS WORK-OUT IS

to *depend* on their lovers to make the relationship better instead of taking the "First Step" themselves. Too often, this leads to a power struggle until each lover refuses to move toward the other. Working out together changes the angry accusatory you-me relationship into a we relationship. Anger dissolves and sex evolves.

WORK-OUT NOTES

_____

_____

_____

_____

_____

_____

_____

_____

_____

_____

_____

ANGER WORK-OUT #21

Mirror, Mirror . . .

Recommended for:
1. *People who have self-defeating behaviors*
2. *People who are chronically angry*
3. *People who want to be good to themselves*

PURPOSE

When your anger has no place to go, and you do not know how to work it out, you experience the effects of self-anger. You make yourself look bad (obese), feel bad (depressed), act destructively (excessive drinking), feel sick (migraine headaches), and do crazy things (commit suicide).

When you are doing these things to yourself, you end up with a "self" that you can't stand. This makes it impossible for you to feel good about yourself—the most important condition for productive living.

Anger Work-out #21 will help you help yourself by making sure you get angry at yourself in a way that causes you to grow instead of self-destruct.

WORK-OUT NOTE

Self and self-anger can be defined in hundreds of ways. The work-out process uses these definitions:

SELF—the identity, character, or essential qualities of any person.

SELF-ANGER—anger that is directed against oneself.

INFORMATION

Knowing Your Self-Provocations

People get angry at themselves for different reasons. Here are some of them:

> I get angry at myself when I listen to somebody else's advice instead of following my own intuition.
> I get angry at myself when I eat too much.
> I get angry at myself for not doing as well as I know I can.
> I get angry at myself when I don't say how I really feel.
> I get angry at myself for making the same mistake over and over.
> I get angry at myself for forgetting to do something.
> I get angry at myself for making a promise I don't want to keep.
> I get angry at myself for getting angry.

All of these examples involve *self-provocations*—events that make us angry with no one to "blame" for the action but ourselves (in contrast to "blaming" others who commit the provoking action such as the lover or boss who insults us). When we encounter a self-provocation, it is essential that we know how to work out the anger it provokes; otherwise we can remain angry at ourselves for a long time—needlessly. If we have a lot of self-provocations, and we do not know how to work them out, we suffer from an anger overload, which will inevitably cause us to be self-destructive. Knowing your self-provocations becomes the first step in helping our self work out its anger.

Helping Yourself Work Out

Self-anger is created when you don't know how to deal effectively with your self-provocations.

To prevent self-anger from happening, you need to teach your self what to do when you get angry at it. The way to do this is to develop a work-out strategy for each of your self-provocations. You can either use one of the other work-outs (which you may be doing) or create a new one. Remember that it must help you work out your anger productively and you must be able to use it immediately. Here are some examples of using the other work-outs:

Self-Provocation	Possible Work-out Strategy
I get angry at myself when I eat too much.	Eat nutritiously. Exercise regularly. (A.W. #14)
I get angry at myself when I don't say how I really feel.	Practice expressing feelings. (A.W. #7)
I get angry at myself for making the same mistake over again and not figuring out a solution.	Practice problem solving. (A.W. #13)
I get angry at myself for getting angry.	Learn to relax (A.W. #9) Use humor. (A.W. #14)
I get angry at myself when I don't do as well as I should.	Combat distorted thinking (A.W. #6) Clarify expectations (A.W. #11)

All these work-out strategies and the ones you create have two important qualities. For one thing, they help *prevent self-anger*. If you *practice* saying how you feel, you are less prone to get angry at your self for not saying how you feel.

Second, the work-out strategies focus on *doing better next time*. This allows you to direct your anger into achieving your goal instead of taking it out on your self. Thus:

- Instead of getting angry at yourself for missing the freeway exit, focus on finding the next best exit.
- Instead of getting angry at your self for pigging out, focus on exercising or making your next meal nutritious.
- Instead of getting angry at your self for yelling at your lover or kids, focus on using good communication skills next time you talk.
- Instead of getting angry at your self for blowing your big chance, focus on how you can get another chance.

The anger athlete does this automatically every time he gets angry at himself by using the productive self-statement:

"OK, WHAT'S THE BEST THING FOR ME TO DO NOW?"

By using this phrase over and over, the anger athlete gets himself in shape for deciding what *productive action* to take every time he gets angry at himself. Thus, anger arousal is converted into energy. The anger athlete also knows that it is essential to help himself immediately upon recognizing the self-provocation. The *sooner* he responds, the *better chance* for short-circuiting the self-anger pattern.

WORK-OUT NOTE

Speed in responding is very important because it enables you to take advantage of the anger arousal and to use it as energy to "correct" the situation. If you wait too long to respond, the arousal dissapates and it becomes harder to generate the energy needed to correct the situation. Thus, if you get angry at your self for pigging out and you don't make your very next meal nutritious, chances decrease that the meal after that will be nutritious, and the chances *increase* that you will pig out again. Letting your self know in *advance* what to do when confronted by a self-provocation is also important because it helps you prevent counterproductive impulsive behavior.

USE YOUR "A" TEAM WHEN YOU GET ANGRY AT YOUR SELF.

Treat your self well

Treat your self with love and respect. *Do* things that make you feel good about your self. The better you feel about your self, the less likely you are to stay angry at your self for long periods of time.

TAKE ACTION

1. Complete the following sentences to begin identifying your specific self-provocations.

    I get angry at myself when (or for)_____

    I get angry at myself when (or for)_____

    I get angry at myself when (or for)_____

    I get angry at myself when (or for)_____

2. List each provocation you identified, and opposite each one write a work-out strategy.

Provocation	*Work-out Strategy*
_____	_____
_____	_____
_____	_____
_____	_____

3. List three things you can do that will make you feel good, and implement at least one of them into your weekly schedule.

    _____

    _____

    _____

THE BIGGEST MISTAKE PEOPLE MAKE
IN THIS WORK-OUT IS

to get angry at themselves instead of expressing anger to the real source, such as an abusive lover, boss, or parent. One reason this occurs is that they fear confronting the source directly. Consequently, they create "extra and unjust" self-provocations. There are few selves that can handle this anger productively. This mistake can be corrected by working out.

W O R K - O U T   N O T E S

_____

_____

_____

_____

_____

_____

_____

_____

_____

_____

ANGER WORK-OUT #22

Becoming an Anger Athlete

> *Recommended for:*
> *1. People who want to become anger athletes*

PURPOSE

Anger Work-out #22 is the shortest work-out but it is the most important because it gives you a *guaranteed* method for becoming an anger athlete.

When you are an anger athlete, you have the work-out spirit. This means that you live the fact that working out anger is a lifelong process, that you are motivated and dedicated to always working out, that you have the courage to acknowledge your anger and the pain that it brings, and that you are committed to taking an active stance to work it out instead of being passively victimized by it. Having the work-out spirit means using each time you get angry as a cue that it's time to start the next work-out.

INFORMATION

Working Out!

The first step in becoming an anger athlete is to do all the anger work-outs. The amount of writing you have done will let you know if you have actually taken action.

Working Out!!

The next step in becoming an anger athlete is to keep doing the work-outs that you are already doing.

Working Out!!!

The final step in becoming an anger athlete is to continue working out every time you get angry.

TAKE ACTION

1. Do all the work-outs you have not done. The amount of writing you have done will let you know if you have actually taken action.

2. Keep doing the work-outs you are doing.

3. Continue working out your anger for the rest of your life.

WORK-OUT NOW!!!

THE BIGGEST MISTAKE PEOPLE MAKE
IN THIS WORK-OUT IS

to think they can become anger athletes without working out. This mistake can be prevented by working out now.

W O R K - O U T   N O T E S

_____

_____

_____

_____

_____

_____

_____

_____

_____

_____

Bibliography

Abramson, Lyn Y., Martin E. P. Seligman, and John D. Teasdale. "Learned Helplessness in Humans: Critique and Reformulation." *Journal of Abnormal Psychology* 87(1), 1978, 49–74.

Allen, Jon G., and Dorothy Haccoun. "Sex Differences in Emotionality." *Human Relations* 29(8), August 1976, 711–722.

Arieti, Silvano. *The Intrapsychic Self.* New York: Basic Books, 1967.

Arnold, Magda B., ed. *Feelings and Emotions.* New York: Academic Press, 1970.

Atkinson, Carolyn, and Janet Polivy. "Effects of Delay, Attack and Retaliation on State Depression and Hostility." *Journal of Abnormal Psychology* 85(6), December 1976, 570–576.

Averill, James R. "An Analysis of Psychophysiological Symbolism and Its Influence on Theories of Emotion." *Journal for the Theory of Social Behaviour* (Great Britain), Vol. 4, 1974, 147–190.

———. "Anger." In H. Howe and R. Dienstbier, eds. *Nebraska Symposium on Motivation, 1978,* Vol. 26. Lincoln: University of Nebraska Press, 1979.

———. *Anger and Aggression.* New York: Springer-Verlag, 1982.

———. "Emotion and Anxiety: Sociocultural, Biological, and Psychological Determinants." In M. Zukerman and C. D. Spielberger, eds. *Emotions and Anxiety.* New York: LEA-John Wiley, 1976.

———, Gary W. DeWitt, and Michael Zimmer. "The Self-Attribution of Emotion as a Function of Success and Failure." *Journal of Personality* 46(2), June 1978, 323–347.

Averill, James R., Edward M. Opton, Jr., and Richard S. Lazarus. "Cross-cultural Studies of Psychophysiological Responses During Stress and Emotion." *International Journal of Psychology* 4(2), 1969, 83–102.

Ax, Albert F. "The Physiological Differentiation Between Fear and Anger in Humans." *Psychosomatic Medicine* 15(5), 1953, 433–442.

Bach, George R., and Herb Goldberg. *Creative Aggression.* Garden City, N.Y.: Doubleday, 1974.

Baer, Jean. *How to Be an Assertive (Not Aggressive) Woman in Life, in Love, and on the Job*. New York: New American Library, 1976.

Baer, Paul E., Forrest Collins, Gleb Bourianoff, and Marta Ketchel. "Assessing Personality Factors in Essential Hypertension with a Brief Self-report Instrument." *Psychosomatic Medicine* 41, 1979, 321–330. Paper presented to the American Psychosomatic Society, 1978.

Bandura, Albert. "Learning and Behavioral Theories of Aggression." In I. L. Kutash et al., eds. *Violence*. San Francisco: Jossey-Bass, 1978.

———, N. E. Adams, and J. Beyer. "Cognitive Processes Mediating Behavior Change." *Journal of Personality and Social Psychology* 35(1), 1977, 125–139.

Baron, Robert A. *Human Aggression*. New York: Plenum Press, 1977.

Bateson, Gregory. "The Frustration-Aggression Hypothesis and Culture." *Psychological Review* 48, 1941, 350–355.

Baum, Andrew, and Yakov M. Epstein. *Human Response to Crowding*. Hillsdale, N.J.: Erlbaum, 1978.

Baum, Andrew, Jerome E. Singer, and Carlene Baum. "Stress and the Environment." *Journal of Social Issues* 37(1), 1981, 4–36.

Beck, Aaron T. *Cognitive Therapy and Emotional Disorders*. New York: New American Library, 1979.

——— *Cognitive Therapy and the Emotional Disorders*. New York: International Universities Press, 1976.

———. *Depression: Clinical, Experimental and Theoretical Aspects*. New York: Hoeber, 1967.

Benesh, M., and B. Weiner. "On Emotion and Motivation: From the Notebooks of Fritz Heider." *American Psychologist* 37, 1982, 887–895.

Bennett, William, and Joel Gurin. *The Dieter's Dilemma*. New York: Basic Books, 1982.

Benson, H. *The Relaxation Response*. New York: William Morrow, 1975.

Berkman, Lisa, and Margo MacLeod. "Coronary Heart Disease: An Epidemiologic Paradox." Paper presented to the American Psychological Association, New York, 1979.

Berkowitz, Leonard. "The Case for Bottling Up Rage." *Psychology Today* 7(2), July 1973, 24–31.

———. "Do We Have to Believe We Are Angry with Someone in Order to Display 'Angry' Aggression Toward That Person?" In L. Berkowitz, ed. *Cognitive Theories in Social Psychology*. New York: Academic Press, 1978.

———. "Experimental Investigations of Hostility Catharsis." *Journal of Consulting and Clinical Psychology* 35, 1970, 1–7.

———. "The Frustration-Aggression Hypothesis Revisited." In L. Berkowitz. *Roots of Aggression*. New York: Atherton Press, 1969.

Berman, Allan. "Neuropsychological Aspects of Violent Behavior." Paper presented to the American Psychological Association, Toronto, 1978.

Bernard, Jessie. *The Future of Marriage.* New York: Bantam Books, 1973.

Bernardez-Bonesatti, Teresa. "Women and Anger: Conflicts with Aggression in Contemporary Women." *Journal of the American Medical Women's Association* 33(5), May 1978, 215–219.

Biaggio, Mary L. "Anger Arousal and Personality Characteristics." *Journal of Personality and Social Psychology* 39(2), 1980a, 352–356.

———. "Assessment of Anger Arousal." *Journal of Personality Assessment* 44(3), 1980b, 289–298.

Black, Perry, *Physiological Correlates of Emotion.* New York and London: Academic Press, 1970.

Bland, Jeffrey. "The Junk-Food Syndrome." *Psychology Today,* January 1982, 92.

Bohart, Arthur C. "Toward a Cognitive Theory of Catharsis." *Psychotherapy: Theory, Research, and Practice* 17(2), Summer 1980, 192–201.

Bonime, Walter. "Anger As a Basis for a Sense of Self." *Journal of the American Academy of Psychoanalysis* 4(1), 1976, 7–12.

Bowlby, John. *Attachment and Loss,* Vol. 2. New York: Basic Books, 1973.

Brady, Joseph V. "Toward a Behavioral Biology of Emotion." In L. Levi, ed. *Emotions: Their Parameters and Measurement.* New York: Raven Press, 1975.

Breuer, Josef, and Sigmund Freud. *Studies on Hysteria.* Translated by James Strachey. New York: Basic Books, 1982.

Briggs, Jean. *Never in Anger: Portrait of an Eskimo Family.* Cambridge, Mass.: Harvard University Press, 1970.

Brown, George W., and Tirril Harris. *Social Origins of Depression.* Riverside, N.J.: The Free Press, 1978.

Brown, J. S., and C. R. Crowell. "Alcohol and Conflict Resolution: a Theoretical Analysis." *Quarterly Journal of Studies on Alcohol* 35(1), 1974, 66–85.

Brown, Prudence. "Psychological Distress and Personal Growth Among Women Coping with Marital Dissolution." Ph.D. dissertation, University of Michigan, 1976.

———, Lorraine Perry, and Ernest Harburg. "Sex Role Attitudes and Psychological Outcomes for Black and White Women Experiencing Marital Dissolution." *Journal of Marriage and the Family,* August 1977, 349–561.

Bruch, Hilde. *Eating Disorders.* New York: Basic Books (Harper Colophon), 1973.

Burns, David. *Feeling Good.* New York: William Morrow, 1980.

Buss, Arnold H. "Aggression Pays." In J. L. Singer. *The Control of Aggression and Violence: Cognitive and Physiological Factors.* New York: Academic Press, 1971.

———. "Instrumentality of Aggression Feedback and Frustration As Determinants of Physical Aggression." *Journal of Personality and Social Psychology* 3(2), 1966, 153–162.

————, and Robert A. Plomin. *A Temperament Theory of Personality Development*. London: John Wiley & Sons, 1975.

Cannon, Walter B. *Bodily Changes in Pain, Hunger, Fear, and Anger*. New York: Appleton, 1915.

Carr, John E., and Eng Kong Tan. "In Search of the True Amok: Amok As Viewed Within Malay Culture." *American Journal of Psychiatry* 133(11), November 1976, 1295–1299.

Cline-Naffziger, Claudeen. "Women's Lives and Frustration, Oppression and Anger: Some Alternatives." *Journal of Counseling Psychology* 21(1), January 1974, 51–56.

Cochrane, R. "Hostility and Neuroticism Among Unrelated Essential Hypertensives." *Journal of Psychosomatic Research* 17, 1973, 215–218.

Cohen, M. Audio tape program: "The Six Million Dollar Seminar." Los Angeles: Cohen Brown Management Group, 1980.

Cohen, Sheldon. "Sound Effects on Behavior." *Psychology Today*, October 1981, 38–50.

Danesh, Hossain B. "Anger and Fear." *American Journal of Psychiatry* 134(10), October 1977, 1109–1112.

Dembroski, Theodore, J. MacDougall, and Jim L. Shields. "Physiologic Reactions to Social Challenge in Persons Evidencing the Type-A Coronary-Prone Behavior Pattern." *Journal of Human Stress* 3, 1977, 2–10.

Dollard, J. R., L. W. Dobb, N. E. Miller, and R. S. Sears. *Frustration and Aggression*. New Haven, Conn.: Yale University Press, 1939.

Draper, Patricia. "The Learning Environment for Aggression and Antisocial Behavior Among the !Kung." In A. Montagu, ed. *Learning Nonaggression*. New York: Oxford University Press (paperback), 1978.

D'Zurilla, T. J., and Goldfried, M. R. "Problem Solving and Behavior Modification." *Journal of Abnormal Psychology* 78, 1971, 107–126.

Ebbesen, Ebbe, Birt Duncan, and Vladimir Konečni. "Effects of Content of Verbal Aggression on Future Verbal Aggression: A Field Experiment." *Journal of Experimental Social Psychology* 11, 1975, 192–204.

Elliot, Frank A. "The Neurology of Explosive Rage: The Dyscontrol Syndrome." *The Practitioner* 217, July 1976, 51–60.

Ellis, Albert. *How to Live with and Without Anger*. New York: Reader's Digest Press, 1977.

————, and Harper, R. *A Guide to Rational Living*. North Hollywood, Calif.: Wilshire Books, 1961.

Epstein, Seymour. "The Ecological Study of Emotions in Humans." In P. Pliner, K. R. Blankstein, and I. M. Spigel, eds. *Perception of Emotion in Self and Others*. New York: Plenum Press, 1979.

Evans, D. R., and M. T. Hearn. "Anger and Systematic Desensitization." *Psychological Reports* 32(2), April 1973, 569–570.

Foster, Randall, and Donald F. Lomas. "Anger, Disability and Demands in the Family." *American Journal of Orthopsychiatry* 48, April 1978, 228–235.

Foulks, Edward F. "Interpretations of Human Affect." *Journal of Operational Psychiatry* 10(1), 1979, 20–27.

Frodi, Ann. "Effects of Varying Explanations Given for a Provocation on Subsequent Hostility." *Psychological Reports* 38, April 1976, 659ff.

Funkenstein, Daniel H. "The Physiology of Fear and Anger." *Scientific American* 192(5), May 1955, 74–80.

Gaines, T., P. Kirwin, and W. Gentry. "The Effect of Descriptive Anger Expression, Insult, and No Feedback on Interpersonal Aggression, Hostility, and Empathy Motivation." *Genetic Psychology Monograph* 95(2), May 1977, 349–367.

Gates, G. S. "An Observational Study of Anger." *Journal of Experimental Psychology* 9, 1926, 325–331.

Glass, David C. *Behavior Patterns, Stress, and Coronary Disease.* Hillsdale, N.J.: Erlbaum, 1977.

Goldstein, M. L. "Physiological Theories of Emotion: A Critical Historical Review from the Standpoint of Behavior Therapy." *Psychological Bulletin* 69, 1968, 23–40.

Goodenough, Florence L. *Anger in Young Children.* Minneapolis: University of Minnesota Press, 1931.

Goodman, J. *Laughing Matters,* Vol. 1. Saratoga Springs, N.Y.: The HUMOR Project, 1982.

Greenwell, J., and H. A. Dengerink. "The Role of Perceived Versus Actual Attack in Human Physical Aggression." *Journal of Personality and Social Psychology* 26(1), 1973 66–71.

Groen, J. J. "The Measurement of Emotion and Arousal in the Clinical Physiological Laboratory and in Medical Practice." In L. Levi, ed. *Emotions: Their Parameters and Measurement.* New York: Raven Press, 1975.

Hall, G. Stanley. "A Study of Anger." *American Journal of Psychology* 10, 1899, 516–591.

Hamburg, David A., Beatrix A. Hamburg, and Jack D. Barchas. "Anger and Depression in Perspective of Behavioral Biology." In L. Levi, *Emotions: Their Parameters and Measurement.* New York: Raven Press, 1975.

Harris, M., and L. Huang. "Aggression and the Attribution Process." *Journal of Social Psychology* 92, 1974 209–216.

Harris, V. A., and E. S. Katkin. "Primary and Secondary Emotional Behavior: An Analysis of the Role of Automatic Feedback on Affect, Arousal, and Attribution." *Psychological Bulletin* 82, 1975, 904–916.

Haynes, Suzanne, G. and Manning Feinleib. "Women, Work and Coronary Heart Disease: Prospective Findings from the Framingham Heart Study." *American Journal of Public Health* 70(2), 1980, 133–141.

Hearn, M. T., and D. R. Evans. "Anger and Reciprocal Inhibition Therapy." *Psychological Reports* 30, 1972, 943–948.

Hess, W. R. *The Functional Organization of the Diencephalon.* New York: Grune and Stratton, 1957.

Holmes, D. P., and J. J. Horan. "Anger Induction in Assertion Training." *Journal of Counseling Psychology* 23, 1976, 108–111.

Hunt, J. McVicker, Marie-Louise Wakeman Cole, and Eva Reis. "Situational Cues Distinguishing Anger, Fear, and Sorrow." *American Journal of Psychology* 71, 1958, 136–151.

Jacobson, Edmund. *Progressive Relaxation.* Chicago: University of Chicago Press, 1983.

Kahn, Michael. "The Physiology of Catharsis." *Journal of Personality and Social Psychology* 3(3), 1966, 278–286.

Kaplow, Susi. "Getting Angry." In A. Koedt, E. Levine, and A. Rapone, eds. *Radical Feminism.* New York: Quadrangle, 1973.

Kobasa, Suzanne, Salvatore Maddi, and Stephen Kahn. "Hardiness and Health: A Prospective Study." *Journal of Personality and Social Psychology* 42(1), 1982.

Konečni, Vladimir. "Annoyance, Type and Duration of Postannoyance Activity, and Aggression: The 'Cathartic Effect.'" *Journal of Experimental Psychology* 104(1), March 1975a, 76–102.

Lacey, J., J. Kagan, B. Lacey, and H. Moss. "The Visceral Level: Situational Determinants and Behavioral Correlates of Autonomous Response Patterns." In P. Knapp, ed. *Expression of the Emotions in Man.* New York: International Universities Press, 1963.

Lazarus, R. "Thoughts on the Relations Between Emotion and Cognition." *American Psychologist* 37, 1982, 1019–1025.

Lazarus, R. S., J. R. Averill, and E. M. Opton, Jr. "Toward a Cognitive Theory of Emotion." In Magda Arnold, ed. *Feelings and Emotions.* New York: Academic Press, 1970.

Lerner, Harriet. "Internal Prohibitions Against Female Anger." *American Journal of Psychoanalysis* 40(2), 1980, 137–148.

Lerner, Melvin J. *The Belief in a Just World: A Fundamental Delusion.* New York: Plenum Press, 1980.

Levi, Lennart. *Society, Stress and Disease, Vol. 3.* New York: Oxford University Press, 1978.

Lewis, D., and J. Green. *Thinking Better.* New York: Rawson, Wade Publishers, 1982.

Lowne, A. *Depression and the Body.* New York: Pelican Books, 1972.

Mace, David. "Marital Intimacy and the Deadly Love-Anger Cycle." *Journal of Marriage and Family Counseling* 2, 1976, 131–137.

McKay, M., M. Davis, and P. Fanning. *Thoughts and Feelings.* Richmond, Calif.: New Harbinger Publications, 1981.

McKellar, Peter. "The Emotion of Anger in the Expression of Human Aggressiveness." *British Journal of Psychology* 39, 1949, 148–155.

Margolin, Cayla. "Conjoint Marital Therapy to Enhance Anger Management and Reduce Spouse Abuse." *The American Journal of Family Therapy* 7(2), 1979, 13–23.

Mark, Vernon. "Sociobiological Theories of Abnormal Aggression." In I. L. Kutash et al., eds. *Violence.* San Francisco: Jossey-Bass, 1978.

Marshall, Gary D., and Philip G. Zimbardo. "Affective Consequences of Inadequately Explained Physiological Arousal." *Journal of Personality and Social Psychology* 37(6), June 1979, 970–989.

Marshall, John R. "The Expression of Feelings." *Archives of General Psychiatry* 27, December 1975, 652–659.

Meichenbaum, Donald. *Cognitive-Behavior Modification: An Integrative Approach.* New York and London: Plenum Press, 1977.

Meichenbaum, Donald. "Self-Instructional Methods." In F. K. Kanfur and A. P. Goldstein, eds. *Helping People Change.* Elmsford, N.Y.: Pergamon Press, 1974.

Melges, Frederick, and Robert Harris. "Anger and Attack." In D. Daniels, M. Gilula, and F. Ochberg, eds. *Violence and the Struggle for Existence.* Boston: Little, Brown, 1970.

Mueller, C., and E. Donnerstein. "The Effects of Humor-Induced Arousal upon Aggressive Behavior." *Journal of Research in Personality* 11(1), March 1977, 73–82.

Newman, P. L. "'Wild Man' Behavior in a New Guinea Highlands Community." *American Anthropologist* 66, 1960, 1–19.

Nichols, Jack. *Men's Liberation.* New York: Penguin, 1975.

Noller, Patricia. "Misunderstandings in Marital Communication: A Study of Couples' Nonverbal Communication." *Journal of Personality and Social Psychology* 39(6), 1980, 1135–1148.

Novaco, Raymond W. "Anger and Coping with Stress: Cognitive-Behavioral Interventions." In J. Forety and D. Rathjen, eds. *Cognitive Behavior Therapy.* New York: Plenum Press, 1978.

———. *Anger Control: The Development and Evaluation of an Experimental Treatment.* Lexington, Mass.: D. C. Heath, Lexington Books, 1975.

———. "Stress Inoculation: A Cognitive Therapy for Anger and Its Application to a Case of Depression." *Journal of Counseling and Clinical Psychology* 45(4), 1977, 600–608.

Oppenheimer, Valerie. "The Sex Labeling of Jobs." In M. Mednick, S. Tangri, and L. Hoffman, eds. *Women and Achievement.* New York: Halsted, 1975.

O'Reilly, Jane. *The Girl I Left Behind.* New York: Macmillan, 1980.

Osborn, A. F. *Applied Imagination: Principles and Procedures of Creative Problem Solving.* 3rd ed. New York: Scribner's, 1963.

Pankratz, Loren, Philip Levendusky, and Vincent Glaudin. "The Antecedents of Anger in a Sample of College Students." *Journal of Psychology* 92, March 1976, 173–178.

Pascale, Richard, and Anthony G. Athos. *The Art of Japanese Management.* New York: Simon and Schuster, 1981.

Patkai, Paula. "Catecholamine Excretion in Pleasant and Unpleasant Situations." *Acta Psychologica* 35, 1971, 352–363.

Persky, Harold. "Neuro-endocrine Determinants of Differences in Hostility and Aggression Between Males and Females." In L. Levi, ed. *Society, Stress and Disease, Vol. 3.* New York: Oxford University Press, 1978.

Pittner, Mark S., and B. Kent Houston. "Response to Stress, Cognitive

Coping Strategies, and the Type A Behavior Pattern." *Journal of Personality and Social Psychology* 39(1), 1980, 147–157.

Pliner, Patricia, Kirk R. Blankstein, and Irwin M. Spigel, eds. *Perception of Emotion in Self and Others*. New York: Plenum Press, 1979.

Plutchik, Robert. "Emotions, Evolution, and Adaptive Processes." In M. Arnold, ed. *Feelings and Emotions*. New York: Academic Press, 1970.

Polivy, Janet. "On the Induction of Emotion in the Laboratory: Discrete Moods or Multiple Affect States?" *Journal of Personality and Social Psychology* 41(4), 1981, 803–817.

———, Arthur Schueneman, and Kathleen Carlson. "Alcohol and Tension Reduction: Cognitive and Physiological Effects." *Journal of Abnormal Psychology* 85(6), December 1976, 595–600.

Pospisil, Leopold. *The Kapauku Papuans of West New Guinea*. New York: Holt, Rinehart & Winston, 1963.

Quanty, Michael B. "Aggression Catharsis." In R. G. Geen and E. C. O'Neal, eds. *Perspectives on Aggression*. New York: Academic Press, 1976.

Restak, R. *The Brain*. New York: Warner Books, 1979.

Richardson, A. *Mental Imagery*. New York: Springer Publishing, 1969.

Rioch, David M. "Psychological and Pharmacological Manipulations." In L. Levi, ed. *Emotions: Their Parameters and Measurement*. New York: Raven Press, 1975.

Rohner, Ronald P. "Sex Differences in Aggression: Phylogenetic and Enculturation Perspectives." *Ethos* 4(1), Spring 1976, 57–72.

Rosenbaum, Alan, and K. Kaniel O'Leary. "Marital Violence: Characteristics of Abusive Couples." *Journal of Consulting Psychology* 49(1), 1981, 63–71.

Rothenberg, Albert. "On Anger." *American Journal of Psychiatry* 128(4), October 1971, 454–460.

Rotter, J., J. Sones, I. Samloff, C. Richardson, et al. "Duodenal-Ulcer Disease Associated with Elevated Serum Pepsinogen I." *New England Journal of Medicine* 300(2), January 11, 1970, 63–89.

Rubin, Theodore Isaac. *The Angry Book*. New York: Collier, 1970.

Rubinstein, M. *Patterns of Problem Solving*. Englewood Cliffs, N.J.: Prentice Hall, 1975.

Rule, Brendan Gail, Tamara J. Ferguson, and Andrew R. Nesdale. "Emotional Arousal, Anger, and Aggression: The Misattribution Issue." In P. Pliner et al., eds. *Perception of Emotion in Self and Others*. New York: Plenum Press, 1979.

Rule, Brendan Gail, and Lynn S. Hewitt. "Effects of Thwarting on Cardiac Response and Physical Aggression." *Journal of Personality and Social Psychology* 19(2), 1971, 181–187.

Rule, Brendan Gail, and Andrew R. Nesdale. "Emotional Arousal and Aggressive Behavior." *Psychological Bulletin* 83(5), 1976, 851–863.

Russell, James A., and Albert Mehrabian. "Distinguishing Anger and Anxiety in Terms of Emotional Response." *Journal of Consulting and Clinical Psychology* 42(1), February 1974, 79–83.

––––––. "The Mediating Role of Emotions in Alcohol Use." *Journal of Studies on Alcohol* 36(11), 1975, 1508–1536.

Sabini, John. "Aggression in the Laboratory." In I. L. Kutash et al., eds. *Violence*. San Francisco: Jossey-Bass, 1978.

Sanger, Susan Phipps, and Henry A. Alker. "Dimensions of Internal-External Locus of Control and the Women's Liberation Movement." *Journal of Social Issues* 28(4), 1972, 115–129.

Schachter, Joseph. "Pain, Fear, and Anger in Hypertensives and Normotensives." *Psychosomatic Medicine* 19(1), 1957, 17–29.

Schachter, Stanley. "The Interaction of Cognitive and Physiological Determinants of Emotional State." In L. Berkowitz, ed. *Advances in Experimental Social Psychology, Vol. 1*. New York: Academic Press, 1964.

––––––, and Jerome E. Singer. "Cognitive, Social and Physiological Determinants of Emotional State." *Psychological Review* 69, 1962, 379–399.

Scheff, Thomas. *Catharsis in Healing, Ritual and Drama*. Berkeley: University of California Press, 1979.

Scherer, Klaus, R. P. Abeles, and Claude S. Fischer. *Human Aggression and Conflict*. Englewood Cliffs, N.J.: Prentice-Hall, 1975.

Schimmel, Solomon. "Anger and Its Control in Graeco-Roman and Modern Psychology." *Psychiatry* 42(4), November 1979, 320–337.

Schmidt, Donald E., and John P. Keating. "Human Crowding and Personal Control: An Integration of the Research." *Psychological Bulletin* 6(4), 1979, 680–700.

Schwade, E. D., and S. G. Geiger. "Severe Behavior Disorders with Abnormal Electroencephalograms." *Diseases of the Nervous System* 21, November 1960, 616–620.

Sebeok, Thomas A. *The Play of Musement*. Bloomington: University of Indiana Press, 1982.

Seneca, Lucius Annaeus. "On Anger." In J. W. Basore, trans. *Moral Essays*. Cambridge, Mass.: Harvard University Press, 1963. (See also "On Self-control," letter CXVI in *The Letters of Seneca*.)

Sennett, Richard. *Authority*. New York: Knopf, 1980.

––––––. *The Uses of Disorder*. New York: Knopf, 1970.

Shor, J. E. *Go See the Movie in Your Head*. New York: Popular Library, 1977.

Shott, Susan. "Emotion and Social Life." *American Journal of Sociology* 84(6), 1979, 1317–1334.

Sipes, Richard G. "War, Sports and Aggression: An Empirical Test of Two Rival Theories." *American Anthropologist* 75, 1973, 64–86.

Skoglund, Elizabeth. *To Anger, with Love*. New York: Harper & Row, 1977.

Smith, M. *When I say NO, I feel guilty*. New York: Bantam Books, 1975.

Smith, Robert C., Elizabeth Parker, and Ernest P. Noble. "Alcohol and Affect in Dyadic Social Interaction." *Psychosomatic Medicine* 37(1), 1975, 25–40.

Smith, Ronald E. "The Use of Humor in the Counterconditioning of Anger Responses: A Case Study." *Behavior Therapy* 4, 1973, 576–580.

Sonkin, Daniel J., and Michael Durphy. *Learning to Live Without Violence.* San Francisco: Volcano Press, 1982.

Sorenson, M. *Slimnutrition and Vitamin X.* St. George, Utah: National Fitness Press, 1983.

Sostek, Andrew J., and Richard S. Wyatt. "The Chemistry of Crankiness." *Psychology Today,* October 1981, 120.

Spielberger, Charles D., and Irwin G. Sarason, eds. *Stress and Anxiety, Vol. 5.* Washington: Hemisphere Publishing, 1978.

Sroufe, L. Alan. "Attachment and the Roots of Competence." *Human Nature* 1(10), October 1978, 50–57.

———. "The Coherence of Individual Development: Early Care, Attachment, and Subsequent Development Issues." *American Psychologist* 34(10), October 1979, 834–841.

Steele, Brandt. "The Child Abuser." In I. L. Kutash et al., eds. *Violence.* San Francisco: Jossey-Bass, 1978.

Stehle, H. C. "Thalamic Dysfunction Involved in Destructive Aggressive Behavior Directed Against Persons and Property." *EEG Clinical Neurophysiology* 12, February 1960, 264.

Steil, Janice, Bruce Tuchman, and Morton Deutsch. "An Exploratory Study of the Meanings of Injustice and Frustration." *Personality and Social Psychology Bulletin* 4(3), July 1978, 393–398.

Steinmetz, Suzanne K. *The Cycle of Violence.* New York: Praeger, 1977.

Stone, L., and J. E. Hokanson. "Arousal Reduction via Self-Punitive Behavior." *Journal of Personality and Social Psychology* 12(1), 1969, 72–79.

Stratton, George Malcolm. *Anger: Its Religious and Moral Significance.* New York: Macmillan, 1923.

Straus, Murray. "Leveling, Civility, and Violence in the Family." *Journal of Marriage and the Family* 36, February 1974, 13–29.

———. "A Sociological Perspective on the Causes of Family Violence." Paper presented to the American Association for the Advancement of Science, Houston, Texas, 1979.

———, Richard Gelles, and Suzanne Steinmetz. *Behind Closed Doors: Violence in the American Family.* Garden City, N.Y.: Doubleday/Anchor, 1980.

Strongman, K. T. *The Psychology of Emotion.* Chichester, England: John Wiley & Sons, 1978.

Syme, S. Leonard. "People Need People." *American Health* 1(3), July/August 1982.

Tal, Ada, and Donald R. Miklich. "Emotionally Induced Decreases in Pulmonary Flow Rates in Asthmatic Children." *Psychosomatic Medicine* 38(3), May–June 1976, 190–200.

Tavris, Carol. *Anger: The Misunderstood Emotion.* New York: Simon and Schuster, 1982.

Tavris, Carol, and Carole Offir. *The Longest War: Sex Differences in Perspective.* New York: Harcourt Brace Jovanovich, 1977. (Rev. ed., 1983.)

Taylor, Stuart P., Charles B. Gannon, and Deborah R. Capasso. "Aggression As a Function of the Interaction of Alcohol and Threat." *Journal of Personality and Social Psychology* 34(5), 1976, 938–941.

Taylor, Stuart P., Gregory Schmutter, and Kenneth E. Leonard. "Physical Aggression As a Function of Alcohol and Frustration." *Bulletin of the Psychonomic Society* 9(3), 1977, 217–218.

Thomas, Elizabeth Marshall. *The Harmless People*. New York: Random House, 1959.

Thorne, B., and N. Henley, eds. *Language and Sex: Difference and Dominance*. Rowley, Mass.: Newbury House, 1975.

Thurman, Judith. "Fear of Fighting." *Ms.*, October 1978, 47–50, 79–84.

Turnbull, Colin M. *The Forest People*. New York: Simon and Schuster, 1961.

————. "The Politics of Non-aggression." In A. Montagu, ed. *Learning Non-aggression*. New York: Oxford University Press paperback, 1978.

Vantress, Florence E., and Christene B. Williams. "The Effect of the Presence of the Provocator and the Opportunity to Counteraggress on Systolic Blood Pressure." *Journal of General Psychology* 86, 1972, 63–68.

Wallace, Michael. "The Uses of Violence in American History." *The American Scholar* 40, Winter 1970–71, 81–102.

Waller, Willard. *The Family: A Dynamic Interpretation*. New York: Dryden, 1938.

Warren, Gayle H., and Anthony E. Raynes. "Mood Changes During Three Conditions of Alcohol Intake." *Quarterly Journal of Studies on Alcohol* 33(4), 1972, 979–989.

Weidner, Gerdi, and Karen Matthew. "Reported Physical Symptoms Elicited by Unpredictable Events and the Type-A Coronary-Prone Behavior Pattern." *Journal of Personality and Social Psychology* 36(11), November 1978, 1213–1221.

Weiner, Bernard, Dan Russell, and David Lerman. "The Cognition-Emotion Process in Achievement-Related Contexts." *Journal of Personality and Social Psychology* 37(7), 1979, 1211–1220.

Weiss, Bernard, Christopher Cox, Marc Young, et al. "Behavioral Epidemiology of Food Additives." *Neurobehavioral Toxicology*, Vol. 1, Suppl. 1, 1979, 149–155.

Weiss, Bernard, J. Hicks Williams, Sheldon Margen, Barbara Abrams, et al. "Behavioral Responses to Artificial Food Colors." *Science* 207, March 28, 1980, 1487–1489.

Weiss, Robert S. "Transition States and Other Stressful Situations." In G. Caplan and M. Killilea, eds. *Support Systems and Mutual Help*. New York: Grune & Stratton, 1976.

Wender, Paul H., and Donald F. Klein. *Mind, Mood, and Medicine: A Guide to the New Biopsychiatry*. New York: Farrar, Straus & Giroux, 1981.

West, Candace. "Why Can't a Woman Be More Like a Man? An Interactional Note on Organizational Game Playing for Managerial Women." *Sociology of Work and Occupations*, February 1982.

ACKNOWLEDGMENTS

This is my favorite part of the book because it allows me to thank all the people who helped me. In alphabetical order, here is my "A" team:

Blanchard Training & Development, Inc., a terrific group of people who have shared my excitement and, more importantly, let me know it.

Ken Cinnamon, who continually contributed his creativity, which resulted in specific work-out titles and a restructuring of the book. He also was a constant source of inspiration. Clearly, the MVP of my "A" team. P.S. That's no B.S.!

Richard Cohen, who helped me "unstructure the structured" and filled my mind with dazzling, thought-provoking concepts. He urged me to do it on my own.

Don Fagin, who took upon himself the monumental task of editing literally every line in the book and who made it possible for my second draft to be the last draft. In just a few days, he was able to find the pulse of the book, doctor it up, and make it better. It was a book-saving operation.

Bill Feldstein, for being the perfect mentor, and one whose style is inspirational.

Ian Fluger, who supplied me with valuable ammo almost as good as my own. Truly, he is a master ammo supplier who delivers in time of need. He also knows the essence of incorporation and the importance of a multivariate approach.

Ron Podell, who listened to all my anxieties and helped me keep things in perspective. He kept me in a good mood. He is the captain of my "A" team.

Kelsey Tyson, who continually helped me keep and develop the vision. He has created and paved the way for numerous opportunities. His belief in my work has given me a tremendous reservoir of energy.

Briana Weisinger, my adorable daughter, who makes me happy every day.

Lorie Fagin-Weisinger, my wife and better half, who always comes through in the clutch. She is the heart of my "A" team and her laughter is my best anger work-out.

Mort, Thelma, and Joyce Weisinger, who taught me the importance of having an "A" team.

William Morrow and Company, Inc., especially Pat Golbitz and Jennifer Williams. Pat's expert editing made the book usable. Jennifer helped me get into the system in a productive way. I am very lucky that my publisher listened to me and let me get involved with the book's publishing details.

All of these people have significantly helped me make this book a reality, and it is my good fortune to be supported by them.

ABOUT THE AUTHOR

Hendrie Davis Weisinger, Ph.D., is a licensed psychologist trained in clinical, counseling, school, and organizational psychology. He is also a Marriage, Family, and Child Counselor.

Dr. Weisinger is the originator of criticism training and is one of the half-dozen experts in the area of anger management. A management scientist, he lectures for the UCLA Executive Education and M.B.A. programs, and for other leading business schools throughout the country. His expertise is sought by numerous *Fortune* 500 companies (IBM, AT&T, ARCO, Control Data, TRW, Warner-Lambert, to name just a few), government agencies, mental-health professionals, hospitals, parent groups, professional educators, and professional organizations such as the Young Presidents' Organization.

Dr. Weisinger's first book (co-authored by Norman M. Lobsenz), *Nobody's Perfect*, was a *New York Times* hardcover best seller and is now a Warner paperback. His article for *The Wall Street Journal*, "So You're Afraid," was selected as one of the sixty best articles ever to appear in the *Journal*'s "Manager's Column" and is reprinted in *The Wall Street Manager's Column*, published by Dow Jones. Dr. Weisinger is also a frequent guest on national television and radio shows.

An innovator in mental-health treatment, Dr. Weisinger maintains a clinical practice as a consultant to A Touch of Care, a residential treatment facility that is an alternative to hospitalization for emotionally disturbed people.

Dr. Weisinger and his wife, Lorie, live in Santa Monica, California. They have a daughter, Briana, and two dogs, Mázel and Shovi.

SERVICES AVAILABLE

Dr. Weisinger offers state-of-the-art (art of the state) consulting services, most notably workshops and seminars in the high-performance skills of giving and taking criticism and of anger management. Both the content and format for each program are custom tailored to your organization's specific needs.

Self-instructional audio cassette and video programs are also available as well as other skill-oriented materials that serve as a follow-up support system.

Dr. Weisinger is also the editor of "Psyche Tips," an exciting and dynamic newsletter that gives you specific concrete skills for utilizing psychology on an everyday, practical basis.

If you would like to arrange for Dr. Weisinger to speak to your organization, or are interested in other materials, you can contact him through:

William Morrow and Company, Inc.
105 Madison Avenue
New York, N.Y. 10016
212-889-3050

Blanchard Training and Development, Inc.
125 State Place
Escondido, Calif. 92025
619-489-5005